ADOPTING THE
FATHER'S HEART

ADOPTING THE FATHER'S HEART

KENNETH A. CAMP

WESTBOW
PRESS
A DIVISION OF THOMAS NELSON

WestBow Press books may be ordered through booksellers or by contacting:

WestBow Press
A Division of Thomas Nelson
1663 Liberty Drive
Bloomington, IN 47403
www.westbowpress.com
1-(866) 928-1240

Because of the dynamic nature of the Internet, any web addresses or links contained in this book may have changed since publication and may no longer be valid. The views expressed in this work are solely those of the author and do not necessarily reflect the views of the publisher, and the publisher hereby disclaims any responsibility for them.

All scripture quotations are taken from the New American Standard Bible®, Copyright © 1960, 1962, 1963, 1968, 1971, 1972, 1973, 1975, 1977, 1995 by The Lockman Foundation. Used by permission." (www.Lockman.org)

ISBN: 978-1-4497-9486-6 (sc)
ISBN: 978-1-4497-9488-0 (hc)
ISBN: 978-1-4497-9487-3 (e)

Library of Congress Control Number: 2013908382

Printed in the United States of America.

WestBow Press rev. date: 05/31/2013

Endorsements

As a pastor who is trying to lead my church deeper into ministry in the foster/ adoption world, I am thrilled to have Kenny Camp's book "Adopting the Father's Heart" as a resource. With gut-wrenching honesty and many helpful suggestions, Kenny walks us through his and his wife's journey from not being parents to jumping headlong into the emotional roller-coaster ride that is the foster and adoption process. Not only will I give this book to any friends or church members who are seeking to foster or adopt a child, I'll make it required reading for both staff and volunteers who work in our foster/adoption ministry. Beyond that, Kenny drives home the most important point of all: that fostering and adopting are God's idea. So when we participate in either, we get to know more of God's heart. Way to go Kenny. This book will be a great gift to many.

Dr. Will Davis Jr., Senior Pastor, Austin Christian Fellowship

Kenny Camp is a man that passionately loves Jesus and as a result, deeply loves others. I have personally experienced his gentle spirit and unrelenting heart, and this book captures the spirit of the man as it chronicles the ups and downs of his family's story. Filled with uncertainty and triumph, this book will encourage you to consider those overlooked in our society. With its practical advice and heart-stirring truths, I strongly recommend the book, based, not solely upon its content, but upon the content of the man who wrote it.

Lance Bane, Senior Associate Pastor, Church of the Hills

"Adopting the Father's Heart" is an essential read not only to families wanting to foster children, but also for anyone who knows a family fostering children. Kenny Camp does a tremendous job relaying information and giving guidance about the

fostering process, but also shows others how to really support families as they are fostering. More importantly, Kenny highlights the comparison of our Heavenly Father with his own role as an earthly father. Finally, once you have finished "Adopting the Father's Heart", you will not only know more about the fostering process, this book will compel you to re-evaluate your priorities, so you will be more focused on others and how you can change lives each and every day.

Kelly Gottschalk, Preschool Pastor, The Church at Canyon Creek

Kenneth writes with honesty and draws a true picture of how the foster care/adoption system actually works. He has a refreshing point of view and in our fieldwork, it is difficult to see the bright side of the child welfare system. However, the Camp's adoption journey - even with its pitfalls - is an encouraging story.

Jen Reichert, MEd CPMS & Kathryn Schumacher, MSW CPMS,
Arrow Child and Family Ministries

DEDICATION

To the family of Chandler Magee: I did not want to use our foster son's real name in the book. I thought it appropriate to use Chandler's name because Danielle was helping him grocery shop the day I received the placement call for our foster son. I know that you all miss Chandler very much. May our story bring you joy in the midst of your sorrow.

THANKS

I want to thank my wonderful wife who encouraged me years ago to write. She continues to encourage and support me as I pursue my passion. I am also thankful for her sense of adventure and willingness to go wherever and however we sense God leading us.

I am also thankful for the staff at Arrow Child and Family Ministries in Round Rock, Texas, who walked with us through our journey of foster care. They were and continue to be a great resource and source of support. We also received much support from family and friends.

Special thanks go to many friends who helped with content editing, proofreading, and design ideas. Thanks also to Pam Gibbs for copyediting.

TABLE OF CONTENTS

Introduction xiii
   1. Are We Ready for This? 1
   2. The Call of a Father's Heart 4

How We Began.. 9
   3. The Journey... 11
   4. Change of Plans 19
   5. The Process...27
   6. Preparation..35

Certified to Foster and Adopt.. 49
   7. Delays 51
   8. One of Five 57
   9. Decision Time.. 61
  10. Major Adjustment 66
  11. Family Interaction...71
  12. Court Hearings 80

Lessons Learned 85
  13. Stay in the Moment...87
  14. Support and Encouragement 93
  15. More Than One Child...97
  16. Selflessness 103
  17. How to Let Go 105

Adoption...119
  18. Parental Rights Terminated 121
  19. Favor.. 124
  20. The Father's Heart Fulfilled 135
  21. God's Fingerprints 141

INTRODUCTION

My wife encouraged me to write for many years, but I always had reasons not to embark on my first book. The biggest reason was simple—I did not think I had anything of interest to say.

At the beginning of 2011, I often felt as if I were in neutral. God seemed to alter my plans a bit, and I was in a holding pattern waiting to see which direction He would point us in. I will talk more about these altered plans later. Having a background in project management and process improvement, I decided to conduct my own personal brainstorming session. I taped white paper on the wall of our bedroom and began putting down all kinds of things I could do while in this holding pattern. My experience taught me to put down any and every idea, no matter how outlandish or unlikely it seemed.

One valuable resource that I had was time. God provided us with the financial means so that I did not feel the pressure of finding immediate employment. I wanted to be productive, as most people do. I wanted to create or contribute something of value.

One of the many things that I listed on the white papers on my wall was to write a book. There! I had put the crazy idea down on paper! It took me some time to give the idea some serious consideration. I had to become comfortable with the idea that I would work on a book project for several months before completion. I also knew that I did not have any experience in writing. Nor did I have a clue about how to get a book published. But after more encouragement from my wife, I began to consistently work on writing. This involved doing some research on how to write and publish a book.

At first, I was not sure what I wanted to write about. I had several ideas, and I outlined a few of them. After a while, I decided to write about what we were living through—fostering a child with the hopes of adopting.

Writing this book was both challenging and therapeutic. On some days, I had no idea what to write, and other days I wrote non-stop for hours. Some parts of the book were hard to write because of past regrets. I was hesitant to share some things because I peeled back a little of my life that I am not all proud to reveal. Other parts made me smile or laugh as I wrote them. Overall, I wrote about what was in my heart. I do not know exactly where God is leading me, but I trust Him with my life and my future. I hope to learn how to rest more in that trust.

My wife, Danielle, recommended the title for this book, "Adopting the Father's Heart." The title has different meanings for me. God has the heart of a perfect father. At least I hope you know Him in this way. One meaning is about tapping into or adopting God's father heart. He desires to protect, provide, restore, instruct, love anyone who will enter this relationship with Him. The fatherly attributes are infinite.

When an earthly father does this, his heart is filled with love, compassion, kindness, and patience. Our heart becomes like God's heart for His children. I believe the best way for a man to learn how to nurture a father's heart is to pursue an intimate relationship with God the Father. I see God fostering in me His Father heart. He is cultivating in me a heart full of compassion for those who are vulnerable and at risk—orphans, widows, and others who are neglected.

Another meaning for the title is the main story of the book. It is a play on words. It is a story about how my heart became open to fostering a young child, one like many others in our communities, one removed from an abusive and neglectful environment and placed in foster care.

I share the story not only from a heart perspective, but also from our practical experience. This book definitely will not serve as a how-to book. I know that our experience with fostering and adopting will not necessarily be your experience. However, I hope it can help you in the process.

Just a few years ago, I would have never imagined that I could be a foster dad. I knew what the Bible said about orphans, but I thought that there were enough other people taking care of foster children. I also thought that it took a *special* person to be a foster parent. And honestly, I just did not feel that I was one of those special people. I did not think that I had the gifts or call on my life to care for orphans. I learned that it does not take a *special* person. It takes someone who has the heart of the Father. I hope that by sharing our story, you may open your heart to the possibility of loving and caring for a vulnerable or orphaned child. By doing so, you will be richly blessed. Both the child and being in tune with God's father heart will bless you.

CHAPTER 1

ARE WE READY FOR THIS?

I t was 2:00 a.m., and the baby's temperature spiked 102 degrees. Danielle and I were exhausted. We had not gotten much sleep for over a week because we were getting up around 5:00 a.m. every day. Now, this eight-month-old baby boy—who had been sleeping in our walk-in master bedroom closet—was awake with a fever. At first, I thought that he awoke because he was afraid, not knowing where he was. He had been with us for only a few days. We knew that he had endured some physical injuries, but we did not know everything he had experienced in his short life. He was sleeping in our master bedroom closet because some out-of-town guests were staying at our house and needed both of our spare bedrooms. I wondered if being in this small room reminded him of something bad that had happened to him.

Standing in the dark and blinking my eyes, I tried to wake up while I held the precious little boy. He was screaming. I was sure that he was waking up our houseguests. Danielle took his temperature again. It was still 102. We stood in the midst of his screams trying to discuss what we should do. We had never had children of our own, so we were not confident in our ability to take care of a baby, especially a sick one!

Danielle decided to call the pediatrician's after-hours number. The nurse recommended giving him ibuprofen and checking his temperature again in the morning. What a classic response! "Take two ibuprofen, and call me in the morning." I felt like a first-time, overly cautious parent you hear pediatric nurses talk about. I probably was overly concerned about this new baby in my life. But didn't she understand that not only were we first-time parents, but also this child was not even *ours*? He finally went to sleep. In the morning when he woke up, his temperature was pretty much gone, so we thought that we were out of the woods. But we were going to have another sleepless night.

That day was uncharacteristically busy. We spent some time with our out-of-town guests before they did some sightseeing. Then I took some other friends to the airport, leaving Danielle home with the baby. To make matters even more interesting, her car was in the shop, so she did not have any transportation. But it seemed that the baby was doing better—or so we thought.

After his morning nap, he woke up with a 104-degree temperature. Thankfully, Danielle had already made a doctor's appointment just in case the baby did not get better. Danielle was close to panic mode by this point. She controlled her emotions as she called her sister-in-law, a pediatric nurse, to get more input. Danielle's sister-in-law recommended putting the baby in a bathtub with cool water in an attempt to bring down his temperature. She also suggested giving him some Pedialite to keep him hydrated. Since Danielle did not have a car, she called a friend to see if she could pick up the Pedialite and drop it by. Danielle also called the baby's pediatrician's office again. The baby became listless and would not drink anything. Danielle understandably became very concerned.

After twenty-plus years of marriage and after not ever having our own children, we had decided to get involved in foster care. It took us over a year to get our certification for foster care. Then we turned down a few placements. Now we finally had a child placed with us, and he was getting extremely sick. We received more than thirty hours of training, but we did not feel anywhere close to being qualified to handle *this*.

Eventually, Danielle brought down his temperature. I finally made it back home, and we went straight to the doctor's office. The poor little guy had an ear infection. No wonder he felt so bad! We were glad that he was not seriously sick, but we had another long night before us. His fever spiked a couple more times, so we were up several times throughout the night to monitor his temperature. We gave him medication every few hours to keep the fever down. He felt better after a couple of days.

I had felt confident that we made the right decision to foster children. We were excited to have this little guy in our home. But, that night—along with the first couple of weeks—were quite a jolt to my routine! In spite of my resolve and excitement, I could not help but wonder if we were ready for this journey.

CHAPTER 2

THE CALL OF A FATHER'S HEART

God is stirring in the hearts of His people a desire to respond to the needs of the most vulnerable in the communities where they live. For too long, Christians have lived self-centered and self-consumed lives. Historically, we have turned our eyes the other way when the needs of the most vulnerable are all around us. Hopefully, we are no longer satisfied or willing to simply study God's Word for the sake of knowledge and gather in sanctuaries for the sake of fellowship. I see a transformation occurring that takes place only when the Holy Spirit moves in our hearts. He is the One who gives us a desire to reach outside of ourselves, to give of ourselves, to sacrifice our comfort and our possessions. Praise God for His moving in us, and praise Him for the response of those who claim to follow Him. I hope we see more of His moving and more of our in-kind response.

Without question, some of the most vulnerable in our communities are orphaned and at-risk children. Caring for these children is clearly something that God calls us to do, and it reflects the true nature and heart of God. Consider Scriptures such as Isaiah 1:17, which says, "Learn to do good. Seek justice. Help the oppressed. Defend the cause of orphans. Fight for the rights of widows." Or Psalm 68:5-6, which says, "Father to the fatherless, defender of widows—this is God, whose dwelling is holy. God places the lonely in families." And, maybe the most well-known verse, James 1:27, which says, "Pure and genuine religion in the sight of God means caring for orphans and widows in their distress and refusing to let the world corrupt you." Dozens more Scriptures reflect God's heart for the most vulnerable in our midst.

When I read different Scriptures that repeat the same basic theme in both the Old and the New Testament, I think that their subject matter is probably important to Him. If I really am His follower, a disciple of His teaching, then hopefully I will do more than just intellectually understand what He is saying. Surely I will live my life so that my actions reflect His heart and passion.

Look at some of the action words in the verses: seek, help, defend, fight, and care. These words call for an enthusiastic response. These words are the call of the Father's heart to respond with action.

So who are the orphans and at-risk children in our communities? According to the Texas Department of Family and Protective Services, the children needing foster and adoptive homes through Child Protective Services are:

- Children and youth between zero and 22 years old who are of all ethnic, cultural, and racial backgrounds and who have been abused, neglected, and/or abandoned.
- Sibling groups who need to be placed in the same foster or adoptive home, or who are not placed together but need to have regular contact with each other.
- Children and youth who have disabilities and special needs, including but not limited to psychological, medical, and physical diagnoses.

According to the Website, *www.fortheorphan.org*, five hundred thousand children in our nation are in the foster care system. More than twenty-eight thousand children in the state of Texas, where I live, are in foster care. That number only reflects the children who are in the custody of the state's foster care system. Many other children live in unstable homes, on the streets, or in non-state group homes. Think about your own community: Do you know how many children are in foster care in your county or city? How do you respond when you encounter a child who is in a vulnerable or at-risk family situation? Do you notice them? It is evident that Father God notices such children, and He is calling us to not only notice them, but also to do something about the problem.

Once children are in the foster care system, they remain for an average of two to three years. Two to three years! That is the average. Do you know what it looks like for a child to be in foster care? Can you imagine what it is like to have someone show up at your daycare or school one day, telling you that he is taking you to a "safe place?" As this child, you may or may not have been the person who brought attention to your home situation. Either way, you probably did not fully understand what would happen next. This person takes you to a complete stranger's home with only the few items you had with you that day. You probably don't have your favorite toy, stuffed animal, clothes, or pet. You may or may not ever see those things again. What do you think would go through your mind that first night as you lay in bed in this strange, new home? Are you really safe? What is this new family like? Are your other family members safe? Will you ever see your family again? The questions must be endless. Many children move from foster home to foster home, experiencing that trauma over and over. It is not the child's fault that he or she ended up in this situation. These are children who have been neglected, abused, or even abandoned. No wonder they typically do poorly in school, act out in various ways, and have mild to severe emotional scars. These are the ones for whom the Father is telling us to seek justice, defend, fight, and care for.

About 25,000 children nationwide age out of the foster care system every year. Aging out of the foster care system means that the government is no longer their legal guardian—their parent. The children were never reunified with their biological family, nor did a forever family ever adopt them. They are now "on their own." The children come from broken families. Chances are many will continue the cycle of abuse, broken relationships, and dysfunctional homes. The Midwest Study published in 2007 by the Chapin Hall Center for Children interviewed 732 foster youth three times from the time they were 17-18 years old until they were 20-21 years old. The results revealed that "compared to their peers who were a part of biological families these foster youth are on average less likely to have a high school diploma, less likely to be pursuing higher education, less likely to be earning a living wage, more likely to have experienced economic hardships, more likely to have had a child outside of wedlock, and more likely to have become involved with the criminal justice system."[1] The government, as the legal guardian, is striving to meet the needs of the foster children even as they transition into adulthood. Thank God our country attempts to provide a system to care for them. However, nothing can meet these needs like a family.

For some time, the evangelical church—a church that places a higher priority on evangelism—has acted as if meeting social needs was the responsibility of the government or liberal churches. The evangelical church's responsibility was strictly teaching the Word and sharing the Gospel. I am glad to see change, a shift in attitude in this area. If we as believers are going to listen to the beat of our Father's heart, we are called and responsible for both meeting the social needs of those who are vulnerable, and for sharing the good news about salvation in our Lord Jesus Christ. Both are mandates in Scripture. Hopefully, the church is waking up to the fact that no government can adequately meet these needs. As Christ followers, we cannot relegate this responsibility onto the state. To do so is to ignore God's call and His heart.

We need to preach and live the *whole* gospel, not just a portion of it. This does not mean that everyone needs to be a foster parent or adopt a child. There are many ways to care for vulnerable and at-risk children. Believers can pray for these children. We can ask God to open our eyes and hearts to these children. We can come alongside to lend our support to those who are fostering or adopting children. We can donate our money to adoption funds or to families who need financial help to foster or adopt vulnerable children. We can get training and certification so that we can provide respite care for fostering families. The ways we can seek justice, defend the defenseless, fight for their rights, and care for the fatherless are endless. We just have to be willing.

---

[1]   Chapin Hall Center for Children. Midwest Evaluation of the Adult Functioning of Former Foster Youth: Outcomes at Age 21. 2007

The bottom line is that if we want to adopt the heart of the Father, we can no longer ignore His heart for the vulnerable in our midst. This is what God has been fostering in my heart. Regardless of what anyone else will say or do, I am compelled by His heart to respond to the needs of those at risk in my community. As you read about our journey, I hope that you will be open to adopting God's heart of a father as well.

HOW WE BEGAN

CHAPTER 3

THE JOURNEY

Our Desire to Have Children

In order to appreciate how we ended up fostering, I think it is important to share some of our journey through infertility. When we decided to begin the adventure of fostering, we had been married almost 22 years. We had never had any children of our own. It's not that we did not want to have children. When we were first married, we decided to wait five years before we started trying to conceive. Even though we were already in our mid 20s, we just didn't feel that we were ready to have kids. We had not known each other for very long when we got married, so we thought it would be wise to spend some time getting to know each other first. However, we had no way of knowing that when we made the decision to wait before trying to have children that we would end up never having any of our own.

It may sound strange, but I am thankful that we did not have children when we were first married. Our first fifteen years of marriage were difficult. We had some very good times, but depression and addiction made me unreliable and unpredictable. At one point in our marriage, we were separated for eight months. I cannot imagine what life would have been like for children living with a father like I probably would have been. I realize that families deal with challenges like this all the time and survive. Who knows, becoming a father might have caused me to mature and change my selfish ways. However, I have a feeling that it would have been a rough time. Not having children during that phase of my life reflects God's protection for our family, both present and future.

In spite of the marital challenges, we looked into fertility treatments twice over the years. The first time we went down that road, we had been married for about five or six years. I remember being very nervous about what we would find. The usual first step is for the guy to have his sperm count checked. To my memory, I never had it done. I wanted to avoid any potential disappointment or pain. I was too afraid to find out that something was wrong with me. Danielle went ahead with some first steps for her. In doing so, the doctors found some medical issues that could have been causing us to not have children. To fix those required surgery, and we decided to go ahead with the procedures. Thankfully, everything seemed to come out OK. We continued with our attempts to have children, but we were never successful.

Because many of our friends were in their early 30s like us, they were having children. At times, that made life emotionally difficult for us. I could not help but think that something was wrong with us. I over-rationalized things, offering some spiritual excuse for why things were turning out the way they were. The years slowly slipped by without us ever getting pregnant.

Years later, after getting back together after being separated, we decided to pursue some fertility options again. We were in our late 30s and early 40s and we were not getting any younger. We both desired to have children of our own. This time around I had my sperm count done. Maybe I was finally growing up! When the nurse's assistant called with my results, her first words were, "This does not look good." I was devastated, and I felt defective. Later, I had a consultation with the doctor who gave me a more professional analysis. The doctor said that even though the sperm count was low, it likely was not the cause for our not getting pregnant. This time Danielle felt defective. She thought that if my sperm count turned out to be OK, then I would think that she was to blame. I do not remember thinking that, but it was a difficult time for us. Not getting pregnant hurt at our very core. We felt deep disappointment, lack of identity, confusion and disillusionment, even a testing of our faith. As we grew older without having children, we often felt out of place. It forced us to adapt our approach to life.

After some prayer and discussion, we decided to try some fertility treatments. Danielle was prescribed some initial drugs, and we had monthly doctor visits along with strict instructions on how to get pregnant. Boy, talk about pressure! But after a few months, we still were not pregnant. The fertility doctor suggested that we move to the next step if we were still interested. The next fertility treatment steps were even more intrusive, invasive, and costly. Danielle and I discussed this option and decided against it. The idea of spending thousands of dollars more with no guarantee that we would get pregnant just did not seem like the road we wanted to go down. We finally decided that if God desired to give us biological children, He would do so, no matter what our physical or relational situation might be. Still, we were very sad. I have a tendency to minimize things, so saying that we were sad is a gross understatement. We were devastated. We were closing the chapter on children unless God decided to give them to us.

Early in our marriage, two different people approached us about adopting a baby. We turned down both opportunities. It seemed like we were never on the same page at the same time. When we were first struggling with infertility, I was ready to look into adopting, but Danielle wanted to keep trying to have our own child. Then later in our marriage, I grew cold to the idea of adopting. I was beginning to think that the reason God was not giving us children was because He had something else for us to do. If that was the case, then why mess that up by adopting kids? As more years went by without us ever getting pregnant or adopting children, the less and less I thought about raising children.

Advantages and Disadvantages

If I could go back and start over, I would definitely choose to have children of our own earlier in our marriage. However, we have had some advantages over the past 20 plus years because we did not have children or adopt when we were young. We have had the opportunity to do many things that we probably would have never done if we had had children at the time. This includes simple things like going out to eat with friends, as well as more complex things like moving to another country for a while. We didn't have to plan vacations around the school year. It is amazing how less crowded ski resorts, beaches, and famous destinations are when kids are in school! Danielle and I have traveled all over the U.S. and to several foreign countries. I doubt that we would have traveled as much with children.

One other advantage we experienced in our childless marriage was disposable income. I do not know if you have checked lately, but raising kids is expensive! When they are young, you are constantly buying new clothes to keep up with their growth spurts. As they get older, all of their activities cost money. Then, if you have boys, they turn into human garbage disposals, devouring all the food in the house and still complain about being hungry. In addition to food costs are braces, extra insurance, education, extra vehicles, and someday a wedding. I know I am not telling you anything you do not already know, but the point is we have not had any of these expenses for more than twenty years. Thankfully, we handled our money wisely so today we are completely debt-free. I am not sure we would be debt-free right now if we had had one or more children we were feeding, clothing, and educating all these years. Of course, not having children is not the only reason we are financially secure, but it sure made it much easier to accomplish that goal.

Those of you who have a house full of children understand the value of solitude, which is something else my wife and I enjoyed. You know it is a challenge when you end up locking yourself in the bathroom for five minutes just for a little peace and quiet. Or what about getting to eat your food while it is hot instead of having to cut up someone else's food before you begin your meal? How many of you moms have had to look in your daughter's closet or clothes hamper to find your favorite blouse or pair of jeans? I have not had to share my space or things with anyone except Danielle. She has a self-diagnosed disorder, PED—Plate Envy Disorder. Danielle eyeballs food as waiters pass by our table and exclaims, "Oh that looks good! I should have ordered that!" It is not uncommon for us to trade plates half way through a meal. I can see how this has prepared me to be a father, learning how to share my food with others without a second thought.

I hope that all of this has not made you wish that you had not had children. It has been nice having my own space and things, but I would have traded all of it for the joy of having children of our own. One disadvantage of not having little ones around for so long is that it made me more selfish and self-absorbed. That is not a good thing.

I can remember people commenting on how quiet our house is. It is true. When you only have two people in a house it can be really quiet, especially if they do not talk much. My personality is reserved. I can easily sit in a room either by myself or even with other people for hours and not say a word. I can remember taking a three-hour trip one time with a friend whose personality is similar to mine. I bet we only said two sentences apiece the whole trip. "Do you need to stop?" "No, do you?" "No thanks." "You're welcome." That is crazy!

Danielle is just the opposite. It was one of the many things that attracted me to her. She liked to talk; I liked to listen. Over the years, I have learned to talk and share more, and she has learned to listen more. The fact that we never had children running around the house talking, yelling, or crying meant that we had to learn how to communicate directly with each other. I wish I could say that we learned how to communicate well with each other on our own, but that is not the case. However, after years of marriage, hours of counseling, and thousands of dollars, I think we do a pretty good job of it today. I know that many couples do this quite well when they have children, but I have also seen couples grow apart during their child-rearing years. I recognize how easy it is to get caught up in the busyness of life when rearing children. It seems that some couples develop a tendency to communicate to each other through their children, if they communicate at all. The dad says to little Johnnie, "Go ask your mother . . ." Little Johnnie runs off to find his mommy, and asks her the question and she in turn sends the message courier back to Dad with her answer and a follow-up question. Then when the children leave home, the parents hardly know each other, much less how to talk to one another. By us not having kids for twenty-plus years, we have learned how to communicate.

Friends of All Ages

Another interesting serendipity of us never having children is that we have developed friendships with people of all ages. I did not notice this as much when we were in our 20's and friends our age were having children. But as we got into our 30's, I began to notice how some friends were younger, some were the same age, and some were older than we were. Of course, most had children. In general, people tend to hang around with others who have kids close to the same age as their own. This being the case, when people wanted to hang out with us, we knew they wanted to be around *us*, not their children hanging out with our children.

We have found it beneficial to have friends of all ages. Those who are older have provided stability, guidance, and in some cases mentorship. Having friends who are younger keeps us young at heart. For a while, I lost sight of the fact that I was several years older than some of my friends. I did not think that I had any wisdom to share with them. Only over the past few years did I realize that I have a lot to offer people who are younger than I.

For about three years, we taught a small group Bible study of young couples in their 20's and 30's. When we first began teaching the class, only two couples had children. By the time we stepped down, there were more than twenty kids among the couples in the class. We did not have any experiential advice about raising children, but we could offer our life experiences, including more than twenty years of marriage. We have been blessed by getting to know several of these younger couples, but it was a little ironic for us to be leading a group of young parents. God showed me through those relationships and others that we had value even though we never had our own children.

Part of the Family

We have been blessed to be included in so many of our friends' lives, including their children's. Many times, it has filled a void in my life. Even though I was somewhat accustomed to not having our own children, I got sad from time to time when I thought about what I was missing. It would not have mattered to me whether we had had girls or boys, athletic or studious, great looking or nerdy. I would have loved being their father, spending time with them, helping them learn, and helping them grow into adults. It was the unexpected moments that hit me the hardest. I remember driving into our neighborhood one day and seeing a dad in the front yard throwing a baseball with his son. I see that all the time, but for some reason that day it was like a punch to my gut. I pulled into my driveway and sat there for several minutes with tears welling up in my eyes, wishing I had a son waiting for me at home to throw a baseball with him. I have often longed to share moments like that with my own son or daughter. What is even more difficult for me is when I see Danielle struggling with not ever having biological children. My heart aches when I see her sad. I know that there is nothing I can do but hold her. Over the years, we have attended many ballgames, recitals, and birthday parties for the children of our friends. Many of our friends' children have called us Aunt Danielle and Uncle Kenny.

We have been godparents, too. Right now we are the legal godparents to four children who belong to some good friends of ours. They are all within five years of each other, so we pray for the parents often! Danielle has also had the privilege to be in the delivery room for the birth of a few of our friends' babies, including three out of four of our godchildren. If we had had our own children, I am not sure that we would have experienced a lot of these things or have been included in some of our friends' lives in this way. I appreciate our friends who made us a part of their lives, even though it sometimes reminded me of what I did not have.

Challenges

Not having children has made some social interaction difficult. Some families don't include us much in their lives. I think it is because we do not have children that can play with their children. Sometimes this is a conscious choice, sometimes not. I think most of the time it is unintentional. I have noticed that we all tend to gravitate to relationships where we have the most common interests or where we are at a similar stage of life. Even though this is understandable, it causes us to miss out on a lot when we spend most of our time with friends who are most like us. I know many single adults who do not get included in other people's lives simply because they are not married.

Another challenge (which affects Danielle much more than me) is baby showers. I cannot remember the last baby shower she attended. She lets friends who are having a baby shower know that she will not attend. Most understand but some do not. It is simply too hard. Of course, baby showers are a time to celebrate, and Danielle is always excited about the miracle of a new baby. However, because she has not been able to have a child, it is too painful to sit in a room where all the conversation is centered on babies and children. Sometimes the ability to have children is taken for granted.

Because of these challenges, when we have considered adoption, a big motivation to adopt was so that we could fit in better. We also wanted to have someone to take care of us when we get old. I know that these are not the most noble of reasons to want your own children or to adopt a child, but I have to admit they are reasons that we have had. When you go for years without having children of your own, you think about things like this. The bottom line is that our lives continued on, each passing year quietly whispering in our ears that we were growing past the childbearing years. At the same time, we were possibly even becoming too old for anyone to consider us for adopting children.

Even though it has been painful and sorrowful at times not having children of our own, I am thankful for how that journey has molded me into the person I am today. I am also thankful for how it has brought Danielle and me closer to each other. It is ironic to me how God used a season of 50 years—including over 20 years of marriage—to prepare my heart all along to be a father.

CHAPTER 4

CHANGE OF PLANS

A s our journey continued, God graciously worked in our lives. Even though we had challenges that brought heartache, they have also brought transformation. A lot of healing took place in my life that also changed what I considered important. During that time, Danielle and I made life decisions that freed us from a lot of worldly entanglements. We have a nice but modest home. We have two vehicles. We have traveled a lot over the past ten years, both for pleasure and for mission work. However, we also lived below our means. We intentionally worked at paying off all of our debt.

Our desire to respond quickly to God's call to give, to go, and to serve motivated us to resist the real temptation from our culture to consume and acquire stuff. We felt a pull to foreign missions. We supported various mission projects and missionaries. We also participated in several short-term mission trips. By the beginning of 2007, our only remaining debt was our mortgage, and we were aggressively paying that down. We both had good jobs that we had held for several years. I was pursuing a career that I was interested in. I was also given more responsibility and an opportunity to achieve certification in my field. Our marriage was healing and getting stronger.

Then in February 2007, we decided to lead a mission team from our church to Thailand. It was our second time to serve with this mission project, but it was the first time for either of us to lead a team. My memories from that trip are as vivid as if it were last week. It was a huge learning experience for me. We were given total responsibility for recruiting the team, booking flights, preparing the team, etc. Three months before the scheduled trip, the team consisted of only Danielle and me! I was about to ask that the trip be canceled, but we ended up with five more team members. A team of seven was perfect. Because I was inexperienced at leading mission teams like this, I foolishly tried to handle every aspect of the trip, from keeping up with the finances to making every little decision for the team, to leading the ministry times. I even tried to make decisions about where we ate each meal. By the time we boarded the plane to return home, I was mentally, physically and spiritually exhausted.

However, when we got back home, we were both ready to pack up and go right back to Thailand for a longer period of time. That feeling did not go away. By May 2007, I was quitting my job, arranging for people to take care of our house and cars, and we were on a plane back to Thailand to live and volunteer for six months. We wanted to see if we were cut out for long-term mission work. Moving to Thailand for six months is a story for another book! When we returned to the States at the end of 2007, we were convinced that we had what it took to be long-term missionaries. We were ready to sell everything and move back. We felt that God was guiding us in a major change of plans for our lives. The desire to be parents was still in our hearts, but we were beginning to think that it would involve adopting a child from Thailand or elsewhere in Asia.

While we were living in Thailand for those six months in 2007, Danielle's father's health began to decline. We decided that we would not make any long-term decisions or commitments to serve on the mission field until we knew more about his health. A couple of months before returning to the states, I began looking into different job opportunities in Texas. I did not want to make a long-term commitment to anything in the states either because I thought that we would be moving back overseas soon. I considered returning to my former employer, but it had begun to feel the ramifications of the financial meltdown that took hold in 2008. Besides, I wanted to find something that would allow me to pursue a return to the mission field within a short time.

I love it when I can see God clearly working in my life. It builds my faith. In hindsight, I can see how God had a plan for us. Because of some changes in the staff at the church we attended in Austin, it was looking for someone to serve as an interim mission pastor. Perfect! We returned to Austin in the middle of November 2007, and I began my new job as a mission pastor in January 2008. The position was a part-time contract job that could be terminated at any time for any reason by either party. That gave me some freedom to continue pursuing long-term mission work overseas. Originally, I thought that I would work as the mission pastor for only one year, but for various reasons it turned into three years. Of course, God knew His plan for our lives during this time because Danielle spent a lot of time caring for her father before he went to be with the Lord in December 2009.

While Danielle focused on caring for her ailing father, we continued preparing for our return overseas. One important way we prepared was paying off our mortgage of our home. Once we accomplished that, we were completely debt-free. This gave us more freedom to go whenever and wherever God sent us. Later we would understand really why God led us to work towards a debt-free lifestyle.

After Danielle's father passed away, even in the midst of her grieving his loss, she was ready to consider a move to Thailand again. My attention shifted to that possibility almost immediately. Early in 2010, I met with the new senior pastor of our church and the personnel team to discuss the idea of 2010 being my last year in the mission pastor role. Then I began researching different long-term mission opportunities again. I could not see any reason for us to not go overseas to serve long-term. Our hearts were still drawn to Thailand, so I was looking into the different opportunities there. Our church had a team of high school students going to Thailand in March 2010, so Danielle and I made plans to go with this team as sponsors and then stay a couple of extra weeks so that we could work with and speak to some different mission organizations. I was excited about the trip because I felt that we were moving again in the direction I thought we were headed three years earlier in 2007.

However, God began to reveal a twist in His plan for us.

About a month before the youth trip to Thailand, a mission conference in our city took place at a church very close to our home. The main focus of the conference was about how to live missional lives regardless of the context. I decided to attend the conference since it was close, since it featured several speakers that I was interested in hearing, and since the topic applied to me whether I was a mission pastor here in the states or was headed overseas as a missionary. Our church staff decided that several of the other pastors would attend the conference also. One staff member became ill and did not attend the conference. Since her registration was already paid, the church allowed Danielle the opportunity to go in her place. This may seem like a small incident, but looking back I can see how it was another detail in God's plan for us. Have you ever been to a conference or event without your spouse and then try to convey the experience to him or her? They understand what you are saying, but there is no way they can relate to the experience. Since Danielle and I were focused on going back overseas as foreign missionaries, having her at the conference with me would make it easier to discuss what we were both hearing and experiencing. It also allowed for us to split up and go to different breakout sessions.

As I read over the breakout sessions to decide which ones I wanted to attend, I noticed that some dealt with orphan care. I also noticed that some adoption-funding organizations had displays at the conference, but I did not pay any attention to them. At least at this conference, orphan care was not on my radar screen.

Danielle and I were enjoying the worship and speakers during the main sessions as well as the breakout sessions. At meal breaks, we would compare notes about what we were learning and hearing from God.

Then the shift happened.

The team that led worship had several members who had adopted children, and at one of the main sessions, the group did a 30-minute worship set focused on how adoption reflects the heart of God. They wove personal stories into the worship set along with statistics about how many children in the United States were a part of the foster care system and were available for adoption. The team challenged those in attendance to consider how the Church should step into this void and meet this need. In other words, if the Church would simply wake up, there would not be any children in the foster system waiting for years to be adopted. In a city like ours, if a couple of families from each church every year would adopt a foster child, no more children would remain in the foster system. I was blindsided by this message. I felt glued to my seat as I listened to the band share their personal journeys in adopting children. The worship began to melt my heart and allowed God to speak to me. But hold on now, I thought to myself. We already knew how we were going to serve God. We were on our way back overseas to be full-time missionaries!

I had not thought about Danielle and me trying to have children of our own for quite some time. Technically, we were still young enough at the time, but it was the furthest thing from my mind. We had been open to the idea of adoption in the past. We had even looked into it when we lived in Thailand. A lot of children live in orphanages or children's shelters in Thailand, so naturally we looked into it while we were there. I had even volunteered at one of the children's shelters. We found out that most of the children in the children's shelters were not available for adoption. Apparently it is rare for a Thai parent to relinquish their parental rights or have their parental rights terminated, even if they were not caring for or raising their child. We were told that Thai parents hoped that their children would someday take care of them in their old age. We had also visited a Catholic orphanage in the city where we lived to inquire of children who were available for adoption. We were given a tour of the facility, seeing hundreds of children ranging from infants to teenagers. I remember feeling overwhelmed by the number of orphaned children. We met with an administrator who showed us notebooks filled with profiles of children available for adoption or recently adopted. I noticed that most of the children that had been adopted were by European and Australian families. We learned that it was rare for Thai officials to approve an American family to adopt a Thai child. Even if we could be approved, it would most likely take a few years for the process to be completed. We would need to complete multiple home visits, and we were returning to the States in just a couple of months with no idea if and when we would be back. We had also looked into adopting from China since we had some Chinese friends. But in the end, we never pursued that avenue either.

So as I sat there at the conference listening to the worship team challenge me, I kept thinking to myself that we had been open to adopting, but God did not seem to plan for us to adopt. While the worship team continued their presentation, I underwent a mental battle about how we had already made our decision. Besides, the worship team members adopted children from foreign countries. I decided a few years earlier that children needed to remain in their home country if at all possible so that they could impact their own culture. My missionary theology influenced my thought process.

Let me explain. My philosophy about international adoption intertwines with my thoughts about indigenous missions. In my opinion, no one can reach a culture with the good news of Jesus Christ better than someone from that culture. If a family wants to adopt a foreign child, then I believe that the best thing for that family to do is move to that country and raise the child in their own culture. I know, pretty radical thinking, but it makes sense to me. So, if we ever adopt a foreign child, I intend to live in that child's country.

Back to the worship team sharing about adoption—

The worship team began to focus their presentation on children in our communities who were in the foster care system. I had never really considered fostering or adopting a child from the foster system. I hate to admit it, but I had always stereotyped these children. They had issues and I did not want to be challenged by their issues. However, I learned that any child adopted has had trauma in their lives. And any child that has had trauma is going to have issues. If I was willing to adopt a child from another country, who would have had trauma, why would I not consider a child right here in my own community? A child here would not have to adjust to a completely foreign culture. I could tell that the Holy Spirit was picking off my silent objections one by one, and I was not pleased one bit by what He was doing! How were we supposed to foster or adopt a child here in Texas and go on the mission field at the same time? I wanted to know that answer! All the people that I had been telling that we were going to be full-time missionaries would want to know that answer, right? I don't think the Lord was very concerned with that objection. I did not even have to go home and try to explain to Danielle why I thought we should do this crazy thing. She was sitting right next to me, apparently by God's sovereign design. He had already taken care of that potential objection, too.

The worship band shared that fostering or adopting a foster child is one of the most missional things we could do with our lives. I don't know how many children were in the foster care system at that time in our city, but it was probably around 1,000 children. As I mentioned earlier, it would only take a couple of families from each church to take one child into their home to meet this need. It was becoming clear to me that God wanted us to look into this. Almost reluctantly, I began to resolve that the Holy Spirit wanted my attention, and I should not ignore it. I am still learning how to listen to the Holy Spirit when He speaks to me as He was in that moment. Now the question remained whether I would obey.

As Danielle and I left that session and walked across the parking lot to our car, I was pensively trying to figure out how to approach the subject with her. Was Danielle impacted the same as me by what we just heard? Was it really the Holy Spirit speaking to me, and if so, was He saying the same thing to her? I still had so many questions that needed to be answered. If she had the same questions and reservations, I knew that I would not be able to answer them. I had no idea how it would mesh with our desire to be missionaries. It sure seemed to me that it would take us in a whole different direction from where we had been headed for at least four years. Finally, I decided to just throw the thought out there regardless of how crazy it might sound to her. While we were still walking to our car, I made a comment something like, "that sure was convicting for me. I don't know how it will work with our other plans or how to begin the process, but I feel like we should look into adopting foster children." There. I said it. Maybe she would say that I was crazy, or tired, or that I had been suckered in by a well-orchestrated plan to play on my emotions. But Danielle did not even hesitate. She simply agreed. After years of not having our own children or adopting, her response left me a little dazed. I have had a handful of experiences when I felt the Holy Spirit was directing my path, and this was definitely one of those moments. One barometer that I lean upon to determine whether it is the Holy Spirit leading or it is simply my flesh is discovering whether or not Danielle and I are on the same page about it. If we are in agreement, I feel that it is a healthy indicator that we are listening to the Holy Spirit's leading in our lives. As we got into the car, all I could think was that this was one of these moments when we were listening to the Holy Spirit, and we were being as obedient as we knew how to be. I had no idea what to do next, but what a change of plans.

CHAPTER 5

THE PROCESS

Seeking Confirmation

The whole idea of adopting a child living in our city seemed to completely contradict the direction we had been heading for nearly four years. Naturally, I wanted to seek God's confirmation in this seemingly drastic change of plans. Because we thought that we were moving in another direction, some things were already in motion.

Our church leadership began searching for a new mission pastor. Danielle and I still had a three-week mission trip to Thailand planned for March 2010. The first week we were going as sponsors with our youth team. The next two weeks we planned to work and speak with some mission organizations. The purpose was to determine who might be good partners with us in Thailand as long-term missionaries. We strongly felt that God was leading us in this direction. In fact, I still strongly feel that He is leading us in this direction.

So how do adopting foster children in America and serving as missionaries in Thailand fit together? I have no idea. We were standing at a huge fork in the road. Whichever direction we went would greatly alter our future, but I trusted that God knew what He was doing. In spite of my faith in His guidance, I had to apply what He had been teaching me for several years, which was how to abide or rest in Him as He worked out the details. I don't mean that I would just sit back and do nothing. Rather, I relied on Him instead of my own understanding.

Besides, I am constantly reminded that my life belongs to Him, not me. Even when it seems that where He is leading me is contradictory to what I perceived as the next step, my desire is to trust Him and remain obedient to His leading. That sounds good, but, man, this can be hard thing for me to do!

As we prepared for the Thailand trip, we decided to put the adoption/foster care discussion on hold. That did not mean that I was able to put it completely out of my mind. It simply meant that I was not going to spend any time trying to figure out how to start the process before our three-week trip abroad.

While we were in Thailand, we spent the first week with our team of youth, then the next week in a village with a Youth With A Mission team that works with a project called Tamar[2]. The last week we met with three or four other agencies in the northern part of Thailand while Danielle had some dental work done in Chiang Mai.

We had a great time while in Thailand, but by the end of the three-week trip, I was mentally exhausted. We traveled through a large part of Thailand during those weeks by van, bus, and plane. We slept in multiple hotels and on the floor of a home under a mosquito net. We ministered to Chinese tourists, to Thai children in children's shelters, and to Thai families in the village. We spent time with several different missionaries discussing their work and the possibility of working with them. I hoped that God would give us some clear direction about what was next for us. Instead, I returned home even more confused. Because of our time in Thailand, my heart's desire was even stronger to return as missionaries, but I also felt that we needed to at least take a good look into the foster/adoption scene before we made any commitments to Thailand.

---

[2]   http://www.tamarcenter.org/en

Where to Begin?

We returned home the first week of April, and after allowing some time to get over jet lag, we were finally ready to begin the process of figuring out how to adopt through the foster care system. Making the decision to look into adopting a foster child turned out to be the easy step. We really had no idea what to do next. Danielle bought a book that explained a lot about the adoption process, so we read a few chapters at a time and discussed them. This helped some, but everything was still a bit overwhelming. We asked God for wisdom and knowledge about how to begin. He soon began to answer our prayers.

About this time, a friend of mine who served with the Austin House of Prayer asked me if we could get together to discuss their ministry needs, so I invited him and his wife over for dinner. Only the guys knew each other, so the four of us spent some time sharing about ourselves. My friend's wife shared with us that she used to work for Child Protective Services (CPS) as a caseworker. For us just learning about the process, she was the perfect person to talk to. She gave us great insight about whether to work directly with CPS or with a private agency. She also spent some time explaining in general how the process worked. They were in the process of finalizing a private adoption themselves, so they shared our heart for caring for orphans.

I had no previous knowledge of her CPS work experience or their adoption journey. My friend and I had never talked about it before that evening. We had invited them over for dinner to discuss how we could help their ministry, but, I have no doubt that God had a different plan for us that night. He increased my faith and affirmed the path on which we were about to embark. The information they shared helped a lot, even though there were still so many unknowns. After our conversation, Danielle and I decided to work with a private agency instead of directly with CPS.

So the next step was finding a private agency. No big deal, right? Well, I was surprised at how many there were in our city. How were we ever going to choose?

A few friends from church had fostered and adopted children, so when they found out that we thinking about adopting through the foster care system, they began to give us helpful information. One friend sent us emails about informational meetings in the area.

We attended one meeting CPS hosted, and they introduced us to some private adoption agencies in our area that worked with them. We heard from four private agencies as well as a veteran CPS caseworker. Besides learning about a few private agencies, we also learned how CPS categorizes children based on their physical, emotional, and social needs. The meeting helped me narrow our decision-making a little bit. I realized two major things: 1) we wanted to work with a faith-based adoption agency that operates from a Christian worldview; 2) we would not be ready, at least initially, to adopt a child with a high level of needs. A part of me wished that I could be a person who could care for a child with high needs because I imagined that not many people are willing or able to do so, but I did not want to commit to more than I thought we could handle.

It is easy to be overwhelmed by the orphan crisis in our country and around the world. Like any other crisis, the enormity of a problem can easily paralyze a person who would normally respond with compassion to the needs around them. However, all of us need to be willing to respond to the need, even if our contribution seems too small. I probably will never care for, foster, or adopt a child with high needs. You may never foster or adopt any child. But there are many other ways to care for orphaned or at-risk children. We need not be paralyzed by the size of the challenge. Instead, we can find a way to care for at least one child in some way. Here are a few ways you can:

- Donate to an adoption fund.
- Provide needed items for a foster family.
- Provide babysitting for a foster family.
- Volunteer as a Court Appointed Special Advocate.
- Mentor an at-risk child. Many children live in children's homes or live in broken families.

As more people do the same, synergy takes place. After awhile, our seemingly little contribution is compounded by the effect it has had on others who decide to help as well. The families in our church who have fostered and adopted through the foster system probably have no idea how they have positively influenced us in our decision to adopt a foster child. Likewise, I have no idea who we have influenced to foster and adopt children.

We learned about another event that was held in a nearby city. The event, called a matching event, included several adoption agencies, along with CPS caseworkers. I did not know exactly what that meant, but it sounded like we would be able to get information from several agencies at one time. That sounded like a good idea to me.

I laugh when I think about how naive we were, or at least, I was. I was not at all prepared for the environment of the event. I was immediately overwhelmed when we walked in. The room was not well lit, so it took a moment for my eyes to adjust to the room. Kids were running and chasing each other. Caseworkers and agency employees were standing around talking to potential foster parents. CPS caseworkers were on one side of the room with displays plastered with pictures of smiling children of all ages and backgrounds. On the other side of the room were several tables with more professional signs that advertised the benefits of each particular private agency. In a way, it was like a trade show that had collided with a daycare.

After signing in and giving those who greeted us faint, polite smiles, we slowly walked into the room. I noticed tables in the middle of the room with overstuffed binders on each one. We wandered around the room surveying each of the displays, not really sure what to do with all the information. I was thankful to see a refreshment table with pizza, desserts, and drinks. That was what I needed at the moment—some comfort food!

The refreshments helped me by giving me something to do while I re-calibrated my overloaded brain. We decided to sit at one of the tables to look through the profiles. There were so many! The children were of all ages, ethnic backgrounds, and needs categories. Most were minorities, over six years old, and had at least some emotional or attention challenges. Some profiles were of single children, but many were of sibling groups. We learned that CPS preferred to place sibling groups together. This made sense to me, but I think it also made it harder for them to be adopted. Initially, we were open to adopting up to three siblings—at least we *thought* we were open to that idea.

I don't know who writes these profiles, but they do their best to point out the positive characteristics that each child or sibling group has. After reading a few, I began to zone out. How would we ever decide on a child? I began to feel very sad as I read the profiles and looked at the smiling faces of so many children waiting to be adopted. I sat back in my chair, knowing that I was about to shut down. I watched all the different people around the room. I noticed the children laughing as they chased each other. I could not tell whether or not they were foster children by just looking at them. Of course, there were several CPS caseworkers and private adoption agency representatives in the room. Then there were all kinds of people that I assumed were potential adoptive parents who were talking to the representatives, looking through the profiles, or standing around eating pizza.

I guess that we looked about the way I felt—overwhelmed—because a CPS caseworker eventually came over and sat down with us. She was very helpful as she asked us some questions about ourselves and answered many of our own questions. It became clear to us that the event was geared toward families who were already certified to adopt. We had not even begun taking classes. In fact, we were not even sure yet what all was involved in becoming certified. I hoped that we had not wasted our time, but I understood this was part of the process of figuring out what to do.

After our helpful conversation with the CPS caseworker, we switched our focus to the private agencies that were present, and we spent time talking with different agency representatives. We gathered material about their agencies so that we could try to remember each one. We had heard of some, but others were new to us. I was beginning to feel that maybe our trip was not a complete waste. We left the event impressed with a couple of the agencies.

Over the next few days, we spent time reading through the material and visiting websites. We eventually decided to attend an orientation meeting for one of the organizations, Arrow Child and Family Ministries[3]. They had an office close to where we lived and had an orientation meeting each month. We attended that meeting in

---

[3]   http://www.arrow.org

May 2010, about three months after we were sitting in that missions conference being challenged by the Holy Spirit. We had not begun any training yet, but I was beginning to feel like we were finally gaining some traction. The orientation meeting was extremely helpful. I liked what I heard, especially the benefits of working with a private agency that had a Christian worldview.

While there are many other very good agencies in our area, we ultimately made the decision to work with Arrow. What helped us make our decision was our interaction with their staff, a common worldview, and the type of children that they predominately placed. Depending on your worldview and type of children that you are interested in fostering or adopting, your decision about which agency to work with could be different.

Now that we had a much clearer path to our goal of adopting a foster child, Arrow would walk with us through each step. The process was not going to be a short, simple task, so having their expertise was very important to our success. Getting to this point had been a little bit confusing and at times a trying experience for me, but we pressed through the ambiguous process. Today, I am so very thankful that we hung in there.

I imagine that we could have done a better job of beginning this process if we had known where to look, but through our experience, I learned about some good resources to help families considering fostering or adoption. Even though the process is arduous and sometimes confusing, it seems to be improving.

If I were to suggest how to get started today, I would recommend the following:

- Contact the CPS office in your county to learn about any informational meetings.
- Do an Internet search for private agencies in your area. Most will have some kind of orientation meeting that you can attend before making any kind of commitment.
- If you are a part of a church, ask if anyone in your church is currently fostering, has recently fostered, or has adopted recently through the foster care system. Not only will these families give

you valuable information about how to get started, they will probably become a vital part of your support network.

- Search for adoption networks in your area. Examples of such networks are *www.orphancarenetwork.org* in The Woodlands, TX; *www.tapestryministry.org* in Irving, TX; and *www.fortheorphan. org* in Austin, TX. Networks such as these are encouraging the local faith community to meet the needs of orphans. They also provide ways of support for families who are willing to be a part of the solution for orphan care.

The best overall advice I can give is to simply jump in just like we did. It may seem overwhelming at first, but it is worth every effort to respond to God's calling.

CHAPTER 6

PREPARATION

Foster, Legal Risk, Straight Adoption

O nce we had settled on Arrow for our training and support, it felt like we had accomplished what we needed to do. In reality, we were still just at the beginning. It seemed like it had taken forever to get to the starting line! We were at the mission conference in early February 2010. It was now the beginning of May, and we were just now choosing the private agency to train and certify us.

One of the first things I learned was that there are three main options when caring for foster children—Foster, Legal Risk, or Straight Adoption. When a child enters the custody of the state, the plan is usually (if not always) to reconcile the children to their biological parents. These children are not available for adoption and in most cases will never be, so families who care for them know that they are only fostering them until they are placed back with their families. This is referred to simply as foster care. We have some friends who have only fostered and are not adoption-motivated at all. They had one sibling group for about four years and another one for more than two years. I really admire people like this who open their homes and lives to children whom they know they will grow to love and then one day will have to say goodbye.

Legal Risk is, perhaps, the most ambiguous of the three. The state of Texas is pressured to provide permanency for a child. In other words, the state is tasked with the job of finding a permanent home for a child, whether it is with the biological parents, a family member, or a non-relative. According to the website for the Texas Department of Family and Protective Services (*www.dfps.state.tx.us*), "legal risk placements are foster-adoptive placements which are made before having achieved termination of parental rights on a child. The child is initially placed on a foster care basis in an adoptive home that is also licensed as a foster home. The intent is for the child to be able to achieve permanency through a placement in a home where he will remain for the purpose of adoption. Once termination is achieved, the placement should be changed to an adoptive placement, rather than a foster placement."[4] The key word here is *risk*. The potential adoptive family is taking a risk that the parental rights of the child will not be terminated. There is also a risk that some other family member will step in to take custody of the child. These cases can take months in the court system to resolve because delays, rescheduling of hearings, and appeals often take place.

Both Foster and Legal Risk placements require a family that is willing to take a leap of faith. The odds of getting emotionally attached to a child and then having to say goodbye are very high. However, the time a child spends in a family who loves and cares for them is priceless. Even though the child will no doubt incur some trauma when they're moved from that family, they will have received stability, love, and nurture during a time of tremendous need.

When we first began our research into adopting through foster care, we did not think that we would be willing to take Foster or Legal Risk placements. Danielle is especially quick to love someone deeply. The thought of her loving a child and then having to say goodbye was not something that we thought we could handle. Even as I write this, I am not sure how I would handle having to say goodbye to a child to whom I opened my heart if that were to ever happen.

The third option, Straight Adoption, is for children who are currently legally available for adoption. That means that the parental rights have been terminated, and no one else—relative or non-relative—was found

---

[4]   http://www.dfps.state.tx.us/handbooks/CPS/Files/CPS_pg_7000.asp

to adopt the child. The child remains in the custody of the state until either someone is approved for adoption or the child ages out of the system. Aging out means that a child becomes 18 years old and is no longer able to live in a foster home.

A family that chooses to do a Straight Adoption through foster care can find out about available children a number of ways. One is simply visiting a state-sponsored website that provides profiles of children available for adoption. The website in Texas is *www.adoptchildren.org*. If the adopting family sees a child or sibling group in whom they are interested, it can have a home study submitted to CPS for consideration. Another way a family can find out about children available for adoption is through their private agency. For example, Arrow sends us profiles of children who are available for Straight Adoption or who are Legal Risk placements all the time. Much the same way as seeing a child on the website, if a family sees a profile of a child or sibling group they are interested in, an adoptive family can submit its home study for consideration. Sometimes a caseworker may suggest that a family submit its home study when they learn of a child they think will be a good fit. Also, matching events like the one we attended bring CPS caseworkers, private agencies, and potential adoptive parents together in one place to help match families with available children.

Again, we were adoption-only motivated. When we first began the process, I would visit the CPS website often—at least once a day—and read through the different profiles of children. After awhile, I would recognize different children, almost feeling as if I knew them. It is amazing how easily I could get attached to a child or sibling group without ever meeting them. After reading and rereading profiles for a few weeks, I decided that I had to stop going to the website. We still had several months of training ahead of us, and here I was already getting emotionally attached to some of these children.

In the state of Texas, a family can choose how to be certified. A family can be certified to foster only, to adopt only, or to receive what is called dual certification for either foster or adoption placements. A family who has dual certification is more likely to receive a Legal Risk placement. The training is the same for either, which makes sense. The child has experienced some kind of trauma regardless of whether they are available for foster only or are available for adoption. Learning what trauma looks like and how to handle it is the same for both situations. As the training went on, my heart softened to the idea of fostering, but I was not ready to go there yet. We ultimately decided to get certified for both fostering and adoption, just in case we decided to accept a legal risk placement. We definitely were not considering fostering only at this time. However, I was beginning to understand how fostering gives a family an opportunity not only to care for an at risk child, but also to mentor birth parents and possibly even extended family as they work toward reunification. No doubt, it is an incredible opportunity to have a powerfully positive influence on a family, but we were not ready to commit to that.

Application

Before taking any training classes, we filled out a substantial application[5] required by Arrow. It included questions about employment history, marital history, other children in the family (including grown children), academic history, military service, previous childcare experience, personal interests, religious background, type of transportation we owned, and health history, both physical and emotional. Whew! It also asked for a pastor's reference plus three personal references. A criminal record check was also conducted on both of us. Anyone living in the home over the age of 14 also had to have a criminal background check. All of that was just for the first part of the application! The application continued with these basic requirements:

- Be at least 25 years of age.
- A clean criminal record for five years and no history of abusing children.

---

[5] http://www.arrow.org/family/christianfostercare/Foster-Applicaton.html

- Have a high school diploma or GED.
- Have been married, divorced, or widowed for at least one year.
- Be gainfully employed.
- Have a driver's license, auto insurance, and dependable transportation.
- Be a legal resident of the United States.
- Demonstrate a lifestyle that embraces the basic tenets of a Christian faith.

The application asked for a floor plan of our house, a sketch of our property, questions about any outdoor recreation, such as a pool or trampoline, a weapons inventory, pets we had, our disaster plan, and which doctor and dentist our foster children would see. It finished with asking for our family budget, including our assets, and our insurance coverage information. I can imagine that the length and depth of the application could discourage some people from continuing the process for certification. It took us a couple of weeks to put together our application and turn it in. Finally, we were ready to begin taking our training classes three months after we had made the decision to look into adopting through the foster care system.

Arrow gave us a list of expectations and additional requirements. After reading the list, we knew we still had quite a bit ahead of us before we would be certified. I am glad that Danielle and I both were committed to this journey. Here is some of the list:

- Complete required hours of pre-service foster parent training
- Health and fire inspection of home
- Become certified in CPR and First Aid
- Obtain TB tests for all residents in the home
- Provide copy of marriage license
- Maintain annual training requirements of 30 hours per year for each foster parent in a two-parent home
- Have a bedroom of at least 80 square feet for one foster child or 40 square feet per child if sharing a room

To become a foster parent or adopt through the foster care system you have to be willing to allow them to get in your business! That is exactly how I felt. Just wait 'til you hear about the Home Study!

Training Classes

The number of hours of training classes required depends a little on who is doing the certification. Generally, it is about 35-40 hours of classroom training. At least this was the case for us. I am sure that the classes and the state requirements changes from time to time, so I can almost guarantee that the specifics would be different for you. However, you can get an idea of what the classes are like from our experience. The topics for Arrow's training at the time we went through it included Child Development; Separation, Loss and Grief; Communication; Medication; Behavior Modification; Strengthening Family Relationships; Documentation; Child Sexual Abuse and Neglect; How to Restrain, and as mentioned above, CPR and First Aid.[6] Not every class is offered every month, so if you took every class when it was offered, it would take about three months to complete the class work.

As you can tell by the titles of the training classes, some of the subjects were not easy to study. The Child Sexual Abuse and Neglect class was especially difficult for me. The trainers were good at giving just enough realistic information to know what to possibly expect from a child placed in our home. It is disturbing to think about what some of these kids have gone through. After hearing some of the stories, it is no surprise that they tend to act out in various ways, some of which are destructive to themselves, others, and property. Many of the children have been prescribed some kind of drug to help them manage the trauma they have experienced, such as anti-depressants, anti-anxiety, sedatives, etc.

---

[6] http://www.arrow.org/family/christianfostercare/Foster-Parent-Training.html

I often left class in a pensive mood. Our drive home was about 20 minutes, which allowed Danielle and me time to process what we heard in class. We talked about what we learned and how it could potentially affect our home. Anyone considering fostering or adopting needs to understand that because these children experienced the trauma of abuse, neglect, abandonment, or at the very least separation, there will most likely be an effect on your family when they are placed with you.

Sometimes it felt as if the trainers were trying to discourage us or even scare us away from fostering or adopting these kids. They told worst-case stories about children who would act out in a bizarre manner because of the trauma that they had endured. If you think about it, a child removed from his home has no reason to believe that he is safe in your home or anyone else's. Many will test you to see how much you will take before you ship them off to the next home. I think the trainers tried to prepare foster parents for these scenarios the best that they could. It would be better to be aware of the challenges and back out while taking classes than after a child has been placed with you. Moving from one home to another is the last thing a child who has been through this kind of trauma needs. The sad thing is that this probably happens way too often.

The training provided good basic parenting skills. Parents of biological children often responded that they wished they had received that kind of training before they'd had their own children. It does seem a little ironic that any two people can go out and have a baby with no preparation to be a parent, but for someone who wants to care for orphaned children, they have to take hours of training. Sadly, this is one reason why so many children end up in foster care. Their parents were unprepared, came from dysfunctional homes themselves, were repeating the same patterns with their children, and didn't know where to turn for help or even knew that something was wrong and that they needed help.

I learned a lot from the training, but it seemed to take forever for us to get through all the classes. When we first began, I still worked as the mission pastor at our church, so I traveled some with mission teams. Other schedule conflicts also came up that prevented us from taking each class the first time around. I wondered if I would retain any of the knowledge that I gained from the classes. We completed the training in about five months. Completing the required classes in five to six months is probably more realistic with the busy lives most people lead.

Sticking with the training depends a lot on your resolve and commitment. I wondered about my commitment a couple of times during the training, but we made it. Five months of training classes, home inspections, and other requirements prepared us for the next step—the Home Study.

Home Study and Certification

I am sure you have noticed how those who run for political office have their personal lives rummaged through. Even if I had a desire to run for political office, I would be very hesitant because of past mistakes in my life that would become public knowledge. Well, our home study felt exactly like that to me.

The home study consisted of three grueling interview sessions on consecutive days. Each session was scheduled for three hours. The first one was with me, the second one was with Danielle, and the third one was with both of us together. If we had had biological children, the agency would have interviewed each child individually as well. This was one of the most intense interviews that I have ever had. Arrow's website states that the purpose for the interview is to make sure that you are ready for the challenge of fostering children.

A caseworker from Arrow scheduled our home study for the middle of October 2010. The caseworker that was assigned to our home study was a young single lady. She had a laid-back, calm personality, which I appreciated. That made the interview a little bit easier for me. The questions in my interview revolved around my relationships with members of my family of origin, both past and current, our finances, our marriage, my personality, my hobbies, and so on. The toughest subject that we discussed was our marriage. This was tough because of the challenges Danielle and I have endured. The questions began innocently and seemed routine. Then she asked if we had ever had marriage counseling.

I want to interject here that before our home study, Danielle and I had discussed what parts of our lives might be difficult to talk about in our interviews. I guess like most people, we had some skeletons in our closets. I definitely had more than Danielle. We wanted to make sure that we were on the same page in regard to how much detail we would share. We both strongly felt that if God wanted us to adopt a child, He could make it happen. He obviously knew our past!

The fact that she asked about marriage counseling revealed to me what I really already knew—many if not most couples have marriage counseling of some kind sooner or later. When I answered that yes, we had, she asked why. When I told her why, she then asked how that had affected our marriage. When I told her that we had been separated for eight months several years ago . . . well, I think you get the picture. We were definitely chasing down a rabbit hole. In fact, I felt as if I was getting caught up in a vortex and had no way of getting out! I wanted to answer truthfully, but I did not want to get stuck on this topic. I could not help but wonder if the information that I was sharing would disqualify us. I knew that Danielle and I had agreed beforehand to be truthful about our marriage challenges, but would she be angry with me for being too forthcoming? I could have carefully worded my answers to make it look better than it really was, hoping that it would not disqualify us, but I had decided that if it were God's plan for us to adopt, then He would take care of the details. The caseworker finally moved on to some other subjects, but I could not help but think that after all the work we had done to get to this point, it was all over.

When she was through with my interview, she told me rather plainly that because of my past and our marriage struggles, the odds of us ever being selected for a straight adoption placement, or for that matter a legal risk placement, were very slim. That news hit me hard, even though I expected to hear it. She knew that CPS would look at potentially hundreds of family profiles for any child available for adoption. Then they would narrow that stack of profiles down to the top three-five families before making their final choice. It made sense that any profile with a "red flag" such as ours would be quickly put aside. Ouch! Even though it made sense, I was disappointed hearing it.

The next evening, the caseworker interviewed Danielle. The questions were basically the same, but she asked a lot of questions about the separation. She wanted to know how things were today in our marriage. Since we did not want to hide anything about our past, Danielle's answers correlated with mine. It just was not worth being deceptive to try to control the outcome. I imagine that we all make an attempt to control the outcome of any given situation. I guess that we think we know what is best for others or us. The reality is that we are finite creatures who have a very shortsighted paradigm. Only God really knows what is best for us, so why not trust and rest in Him to do what is best for us? Of course, that sounds easy, but we all know it is hard. Danielle and I were doing our best to rest in Him and trust Him with the outcome.

Danielle's interview was not nearly as long as mine. I guess the caseworker did not see any need to pursue any subjects like she did in my interview.

After Danielle's night of interviewing, we were talking about how things went and were licking our wounds a bit. I only remember one thing that Danielle said to me. She told me that she was proud of me for being honest and authentic during my interview. That meant a lot to me because I knew how strongly she desired to adopt a child. A lot of wives in that situation would have been upset that I did not paint a better picture to help that desire become a reality. Instead, Danielle appreciated my character. That speaks loudly about her character as well.

The third night, the caseworker interviewed us together. The questions were more on parenting styles, which for us was all theoretical. This line of questioning was a lot easier on us than the two nights of individual interviews. Still, we were mentally exhausted when the third night of interviews was over. The caseworker reemphasized that because of my past, it would be very slim odds for us to ever be selected for a straight adoption placement or for a legal risk placement. She said it was possible, but we could wait for years before being selected. Even though this was hard to hear, God had already been opening our hearts to fostering.

The caseworker did offer some encouragement, though. She let us know that if a child placed with us as a foster placement ever became legally free for non-relative adoption, we would be given first consideration. I appreciated her encouragement. I may have given up were it not for that small glimmer of hope.

She was also very kind in letting us know that she appreciated our honesty about who we were. She shared how she was used to hearing stories that sounded too good to be true. Our story surely was not one of those! It helped me to hear her encouraging words. Regardless of what happened with adoption, I could feel good about being truthful. However, we still felt uneasy about fostering, but we were not willing to wait for years to be selected for a straight adoption or legal risk placement.

Another option for us was to do respite care for foster families while we waited for a straight adoption or legal risk placement. Respite care simply means long-term babysitting. At the time of our certification, any childcare for a foster child that was for longer than 72 hours required a certified foster parent. Providing respite care for foster families would give us a chance to care for foster children without the full commitment and attachment. It also would give us a chance to meet some children who were in the foster care system. One of our friends from church met their adopted son this way.

Our trainers at Arrow reminded us that we were the adults. We needed to be the ones who were mature enough to handle these tough situations. That included being willing to put our hearts out there to foster, knowing that the child or children would probably only be with us for a short period of time. That meant that there would likely be some pain involved, especially when it came time for the child to return to his biological family or be adopted by another family. The reality is that there are hundreds—if not thousands—of vulnerable children in the foster care system. These children need well-adjusted families where they will be loved and safe. They need an environment where they are able to process the trauma that is happening in their life, hopefully coming through it with some sanity intact. When the focus is on the well-being of these children instead of me as an adult, it changes my concern for how I am able to handle the trauma that it may bring me.

Danielle and I had come a long way in less than a year. When we began, we were more focused on ourselves, even though we were considering adopting an orphaned child. Yet God was gently massaging our hearts. We were considering the idea of opening our hearts to an at-risk child who needed us. We would do this knowing full well that our hearts most likely would be hurt one day, but we were willing to trust that God would graciously protect our hearts or give us what we needed when it came time to let go of a foster child. God was fostering a genuine desire in me to be a father to the fatherless. So we finally decided to go for it and tell our agency that we were open to fostering.

After our home study, it took about two months for Arrow to complete our profile and legally certify us. I was surprised at how long it took them to finalize everything. From time to time, I hear stories about foster families that are not much better than the family that the child was removed from, and based on our long, detailed certification process, I wonder how they ever became approved to be foster parents.

We finally received our official certificate in the mail in mid-January 2011. The Texas Department of Protective and Regulatory Services issued the certificate stating the following:

> "This duly authorized Child-Placing Agency (Arrow Child and Family Ministries) attests to the fact that the person or persons listed meet the appropriate minimum standards in compliance with Human Resources Code, Chapter 42 and issues this Agency Home Verification To: "our names and address"
>
> Foster/Adopt/Respite Child Care Services: Basic, Moderate, Specialized
>
> For the care of: 3 Children, Male and Female, Ages 0-17
>
> Granted this the 15th day of January 2011"

We proudly displayed the framed certificate on a table in our foyer for everyone to see as soon as they walk into our home. We are required to have it visibly displayed anyway!

So here we were nearly one year after that mission conference where we felt the Holy Spirit challenge us. It seemed to have taken a lot longer than I originally expected, but we really had accomplished a lot during that year. We went from not knowing how to get started to being certified foster parents. Still, if I had known in the beginning that it was going to take a whole year to get to this point, I don't know if I would have agreed to do it.

I still had lots of questions and concerns. I had no idea how this was going to fit with our desire to be on the mission field. I got that question a lot from our friends, too, but I continued to let God deal with how it was going to work out if He wanted us to do both. By this time, I had officially resigned from my mission pastor position and had only a few more weeks left before my last day on the job. I was quickly moving into a season of the unknown for me. Thank God He had been preparing me for the journey. Even though I had no idea what exactly was ahead of us, I was willing to buckle my seatbelt and go along for the ride.

CERTIFIED TO FOSTER AND ADOPT

CHAPTER 7

DELAYS

Always Something

As soon as our home study was approved and we were certified in January 2011, we began to receive calls for fostering children. As you read, our license certified us to foster up to three children, male or female, ages 0-17. We had written down those parameters on our application at the very beginning of the process. Now think about that for a second with me. We had never had children of our own, and we were going to begin our foster experience with three children of any age? What were we thinking?

When we filled out our application, we did not know for sure what we wanted to do or what we could handle. Our training classes and other more experienced foster parents helped us figure out how we wanted to begin. We decided to narrow our parameters a little bit. We decided that the optimum age for us would be 4-10 years old. We were open to a younger child, and we were open to a boy who might be a little bit older. At first, we were open to a sibling group, but then we decided that it would be wise for our first foster placement to be a single child instead of a sibling group. Now that we better understood what fostering would be like, we were not sure if we could handle more than one traumatized child at a time.

We did not do a good job of communicating our new parameters to Arrow, so the first couple of calls were for kids whom we felt were outside of the parameters that we had decided upon. Even though it was very hard to say no, we wanted to trust our decision that we had made in a non-emotional moment. When a phone call for a placement comes, you only have a few minutes to decide whether or not you will take the child. That decision made in a brief moment will have long-lasting effects on both the foster family and the foster child. After you welcome him into your home, you really have no idea how long he will be with you. The last thing anyone wants to see happen is for a foster child to move from home to home. I know that this happens, and sometimes it cannot be prevented. However, all too often a child is removed from a foster home simply because the foster family decided that they did not want to care for the child any longer. All that does is add to the trauma experienced by that child. How can he not begin to wonder if something is wrong with him? So we may have been a little over cautious at first in turning down a few placements, but I wanted to be as sure as possible that it was a good fit.

Some of the calls we turned down because of our schedule. For example, I was in Thailand for the first two weeks of February 2011 with a mission team from our church. It was my last official trip as the mission pastor of our church, so I wanted to be on the team, but this left Danielle at home alone for a couple of weeks. Of course, this was not the first time that I had traveled overseas without her, but we were not certified foster parents at the time. I think Danielle felt confident that she could handle a placement while I was gone, and I am sure she could have. If it would not have been the very first one, I may have been more open to it. I asked her to not take a placement while I was gone. I did not want to be on the other side of the world if the placement was a challenge; nor did I want to miss our first placement.

Sure enough, Danielle got a call about a placement for two children while I was in Thailand. In spite of the fact that we had decided to take only one foster child for our first placement and I was out of the country, it was still hard for her to turn down. After I returned from Thailand, we did have one or two more placement calls, but there always seemed to be something else that caused us to turn down the opportunities.

Even though the delay was beginning to bother me, looking back, I think it was good for me to not have a placement right away. I needed some time to process through my transition off the staff of our church. Of course, I thought it was so we could begin our preparation to move back overseas as missionaries. I was OK with our decision to foster some children with the hopes of adopting, but I needed to be doing something else as well. Even though we had been working on getting our certification for about a year, I had not prepared well for my transition. I was unsure about what I wanted to be doing while we were fostering children. I knew for sure that I did not want to wander aimlessly for an extended amount of time. So the delay in accepting a placement allowed time for me to process through these thoughts.

Danielle and I spent three days at the beginning of March 2011 fasting and praying. I wanted to seek God about our future. If we were going to stay in the States for a while, I wanted to find out how to still have an impact both locally and globally. I also wanted to be as ready emotionally and spiritually as possible for when we did accept a foster placement. Those three days were wonderful. We put down on paper anything that came to our minds that we thought we might do with our time. Some ideas were way out there. Here are a few of the ideas:

- Sell everything and travel the world working with different mission organizations.
- Move to the beach.
- Go back to school.
- Start a bakery.

No idea was too crazy to write down on the paper. One of the ideas was for me to write a book. We also decided that we should take what could be our last vacation without children for some time.

So where did we decide to go? We went to Europe for three weeks! I know, you are probably beginning to wonder if these guys were ever serious about fostering. Even though it would further delay us getting a foster placement, we thought the timing made sense. We both had the time. We had the financial means to go. We had talked about this trip for a long time. And if by the grace of God we ended up adopting a child, at our age this really could have been our last chance to go. So again we put fostering on hold until we got back from Europe.

A couple of weeks before we went to Europe, we babysat the two youngest of our godchildren for four days. At the time, they were little over two and four years old. It was the first time for us to have a couple of young children in our home 24/7 for more than one day in quite a while. They had tons of energy and wanted to play all the time with their Uncle Kenny and Aunt Danielle. I have to be honest that I was exhausted by the time their parents got home! After they left, I wrote in my journal that I was unsure of my ability to foster or adopt any children, regardless of their age. I felt my age in trying to keep up with these young ones. It definitely was a confirmation for me that we should start out fostering one child instead of a sibling group.

While our godchildren were with us, we got yet another call for a foster placement. I guess that we had not informed Arrow yet of our plan to be gone for three weeks. Once more, we turned down the placement. I doubt we would have taken the placement while our godchildren were with us anyway. Not only did we have our hands full with them, but I also would not have wanted to take the risk of something happening with them. No one ever knows how children will react to the trauma they are experiencing. Sometimes, they cause harm to another person. So either way, we would have turned down this placement.

Families that have other children need to take their biological children's safety and opinions into consideration when they think about fostering. It is wise to think about your family dynamics before fostering. If your children are old enough, they should have input into the decision to foster. It is cool when biological children encourage their parents to foster or adopt. This happened to a good friend of mine. He has two teenage boys who had gotten to know a schoolmate who was a foster child. The young teenager who was a foster child had been in the foster system for several years. When my friend's sons understood what it meant to be a foster child, they asked their parents why their friend could not become a part of their family. As a parent, how do you say no to that? I love the pure heart displayed by these two young men and how they have welcomed a new brother into their family.

I am thankful that we took the opportunity to go to Europe. I needed to get away and decompress, and we had a great time. However, by the time we got back to Austin, it was the second week of May. It had now been nearly four months since we had been certified, and we still had not accepted any placements. We thought that after we got back from Europe we would soon get a call for a foster placement. Before we left for Europe, it seemed as if we were getting called each week. Now for once, we did not have anything in the foreseeable future that would keep us from accepting a placement of a child who fit our parameters. After three weeks went by without hearing anything, Danielle emailed a trainer at Arrow to ask why we were not getting any calls. She reassured us that it was very normal. Sometimes they have several children to place, and other times they have very few.

No More Reasons to Delay

Those three weeks, when we were finally completely ready to accept a foster placement seemed like forever to me. Apparently, I was still a little fragile in our decision to foster and adopt. I began to rehash our plan in my mind. I wondered if maybe we were supposed to simply wait for a straight adoption to come our way even though that was a long shot. I also wondered, once again, if maybe we were really supposed to return to the mission field now rather than later. Every time we had gotten an opportunity to foster, there seemed to be some reason to turn it down. We also had some family members who were asking us why we wanted to foster or adopt. I got the idea that they thought we were too old or not cut out for raising children. I think they were only concerned for our well-being, but their questions only served to feed my doubts.

Thankfully, most of our friends and family were excited about our adventure. They encouraged us through the whole process. I needed this encouragement because my second-guessing was affecting other areas of my life. If we were to decide not to foster or adopt, then that opened up all kinds of options again.

The more time that went by without us accepting a foster placement, the more I questioned God if this was what we were supposed to do. Maybe I had been hearing God wrong, or maybe He was testing me the way He tested Abraham to see if I would trust Him even when it did not make sense. Maybe I really was too old and not cut out to be a father.

I was very close to talking to Danielle about letting this idea go and looking into going onto the mission field sooner rather than later when things began to change.

CHAPTER 8

ONE OF FIVE

While she was away traveling with her mother, Danielle got a call one day for a placement for two boys. Even though it was a couple of boys, she gave me a call to discuss whether or not to accept the placement. After talking it through, we decided one more time to decline the placement. We declined because a few weeks after we got back from Europe, we had received an email informing us that we were being considered for adopting a 12-year-old boy! We declined the foster placement of the two boys because we did not think that we could potentially go from no children to three boys overnight. I think it was a wise decision, but once again a tough one. For us to be in consideration for a straight adoption placement this soon was a complete surprise. We had submitted our profile on a handful of children after being certified in January, but as we were told after our home study, it was going to be a long shot for us to ever be selected. Now we were possibly going to adopt without ever fostering a child.

Quite frequently, Arrow sends to certified families emails that contain profiles of Legal Risk children, those who may become available for adoption, and Legally Free, those presently available for adoption. These emails were being sent to Danielle. She would read them, and if she thought that the children fit our parameters, she would forward them on to me to consider. Between January and May 2011, we had agreed upon seven or eight profiles of children who could have been possibilities. When we agreed on a child, we would ask Arrow to send our profile to the appropriate CPS caseworker. We never heard anything if we were not selected. Wondering if we would be selected and never hearing anything at all could be nerve-racking. I decided that whenever we sent in our profile, I would not look at the child's profile anymore to do my best to forget about it. The last thing I wanted to do was to get attached to all these children with little or no possibility of ever being selected to be their dad. Even if we had a stellar past, the process could take a long time. I decided to trust God by doing my best not to stress out each time we sent in our information.

The 12-year-old boy we were hoping to adopt was on the upper end of the age range that we felt comfortable considering. His profile described a boy who was easy-going, liked to laugh, and enjoyed people. He was going into sixth grade and wanted to play sports at school. He especially enjoyed basketball and football. His current foster family reported that he was a great kid with no behavioral issues. CPS was looking for a family who would encourage his interest in sports and other school activities. They said that he would fit in with a family with children or without children. It all sounded like a great fit for our family, so Danielle requested that our profile be sent in, and as I had hoped, I quickly forgot about it. A couple of weeks later, we were really surprised to hear that we were one of five families being considered to adopt this 12-year-old boy.

This was new territory for us. When we were taking our training classes, we were told to put together a photo album showing our family, extended family, and friends, but we had not done this because we were really not expecting to be considered for a straight adoption placement. Now that we were being considered to adopt, we needed to get one together quickly. We made a digital photo album so we could share it with the different caseworkers. We gathered pictures of our family and friends, and I picked out several pictures that told a little bit of our story. Since we enjoy traveling, we had pictures from all over the world. This was a fun project for me to work on. I could not help but become hopeful as I put the album together.

The caseworker from Arrow who was going to represent us with CPS emailed us several clarifying questions she had after reviewing our home study. As she put it, "I need to be even more personal than the caseworker that did your home study." Great! She asked more questions about Danielle's relationship with her father, about her job, and about how Danielle and I handled ourselves when we were arguing. She also wanted to know more about my current relationship with my mother. And sure enough, she wanted to know more about the counseling I had received in the past. If I had not had a conviction about God's call to care for orphaned children, I would have never gone through all the questions. We answered her questions honestly and as best as we knew how. We still wanted to be authentic. If God wanted us to be this boy's parents, then we knew it would be so, regardless of the blemishes on our home study.

I knew it would be a long shot for us to be selected, but I could not help but think about what it would be like to have a 12-year-old son beginning middle school. I have to admit that I was looking forward to having a son who enjoyed sports. Also, we have several friends with middle and high school age kids, so I could not help but think about how I would enjoy doing things together with other families with similar age children. I don't know how anyone could avoid dreaming about adopting this child.

Since this was the first time for us, we did not know how the process would proceed. We learned that CPS would meet the caseworker representing each of the five families all at one time, and then they would make a decision. The caseworker emailed us after the meeting with CPS. She confirmed that there were five families that CPS was considering, so the competition was "super thick." All the families sounded "pretty great" to her. Next we waited to hear back from CPS to find out if they had selected us. It reminded me of all these reality shows like "Survivor" that are popular now. It could make for good TV drama interviewing each of the families being considered. Each would state their case for why they thought they would be the best family. Some would be all anxious or crying from the stress; others would be stoic, acting like they were all cool. OK, producers, remember that you got the idea here!

Later that day we got another email from our caseworker to let us know that we had not been selected. It was disappointing even though we expected it. She passed on some comments from the CPS caseworker that was encouraging: "She was really interested in you guys and loved your Family Book. She didn't have to say that." It did help to hear those words that were in such contrast to what was still ingrained in my head from our home study: "You will probably never be considered for straight adoption."

In the past, I have struggled with replaying negative comments over and over in my head, allowing them to influence how I view myself. I don't do this nearly as much as I have in the past, partly because I have done better at embracing the truth of who I am in Christ. Still, hearing unsolicited, positive comments from someone I did not know at all was absolutely up-lifting.

A couple days afterward, I wrote in my journal, "Over the last few days and especially after hearing that we were not selected to adopt the 12-year-old boy, I have been thinking more about moving back to Thailand. When it comes to fostering and adopting, Danielle and I are being as obedient as we know how to the call of Scripture to care for the orphan. When it comes to Thailand, we both feel that not only is it about obedience to Scripture, but we also feel a strong pull to go."

I was disappointed that CPS did not select us to adopt this 12-year-old boy. Months had gone by as we turned down placement after placement.

Then, less than a week after making that journal entry, I took a call from Arrow about yet another foster placement.

CHAPTER 9

DECISION TIME

Monday, June 20, 2011. Mondays were hard for me after resigning from the church staff in February 2011, so I made sure that I had a full schedule on Mondays. The week before, on the 14th, we had heard that we were not selected to adopt the 12-year-old boy. Danielle's uncle passed away that same day. Needless to say, I was not on an emotional high. We went to Houston on Friday, June 17th to attend the funeral for Danielle's uncle. We made a day trip out of it, so we had plenty of road time to talk about things. Just a couple days earlier we had turned down another foster placement.

Mentally, I was really beginning to make a shift. I was thinking more and more about pursuing a different path. I began that Monday, June 20, by meeting with a guy to discuss an investment opportunity in Haiti. It was an opportunity to invest in a cement block company that also had some distinct mission opportunities. I had been exploring different businesses as mission opportunities, so I was interested in talking with this guy.

I had also decided to begin working on some home improvement projects. After lunch, I went to a home improvement store and bought 300 square feet of ceramic tile for our kitchen and breakfast area. It was a scorching hot and dry summer, and it was about 110 degrees outside that day. I worked for about an hour unloading the tile into my garage, then went inside to cool off. I was sitting at our kitchen table drinking an ice-cold glass of water and reading some emails when I got a call from Arrow about another foster placement. I really did not feel like taking the call or listening to them describe who they wanted to place. I came so very close to not taking the call, but I decided I could politely listen and then turn it down. Danielle was not even at home. She had gone to help a friend do some grocery shopping.

Being where I was mentally at this point, especially on the heels of being turned down on the adoption opportunity, it would have been very easy for me to tell them that we were not interested, but I was feeling a little awkward about turning down so many placement requests already. I also knew that we did not have anything on our calendar for the foreseeable future that would make it difficult to foster a child for a while. So I listened to the information that the caseworker gave me about the child.

It is not uncommon for the caseworkers to have very little information about a child that CPS is trying to place. This is especially true for a first-time placement. Sometimes the information that is given is not even accurate because information gets mixed up as it is passed from person to person. The limited information that she shared with me about this placement was that he was an eight-month-old Caucasian boy. He had sustained some physical injuries, and CPS was removing him from the home as we spoke.

Immediately my head began to spin. I knew that she needed to have an answer quickly so that they could assure a foster home for this baby. Danielle and I had discussed being open to taking a child who was this young, but our home was not prepared for that age at all. What I mean is that we had nothing in our home for a child of this age except for a portable Pack and Play. Our focus was more on the 4 to 10-year-old age. But for the first time since being certified, there was no other reason not to accept the placement of this child.

Danielle and I had agreed that if either of us took a call and could not reach the other, we could accept the placement as long as the child fit the parameters we had set. However, being in that moment of needing to make a decision, being in the mindset that I was in, and knowing that the child was very young, I really wanted to make this decision with Danielle.

I asked the caseworker if I could have a few minutes to try and reach Danielle, which she granted. I had about 10 minutes to get hold of Danielle, discuss the placement, make a decision, and then get back to the caseworker. I knew that Danielle hardly ever heard her cell phone when she was in a place like a restaurant or the grocery store, but I tried anyway. I called her about 10 times in about three minutes. I really wanted to discuss it with Danielle before I made a decision, but it looked like that was not going to happen. I did not have the phone number of the friend that Danielle was helping, so I did not think I had any other way of getting in touch with Danielle.

Hesitantly, I decided that I would accept the placement, primarily because the Arrow caseworker felt like it would be for a short time, possibly for only a week or two. I called Arrow back and accepted the placement. After thanking us for accepting the placement, they informed me that the CPS caseworker would be bringing him to our home in a couple of hours. An Arrow caseworker called shortly afterward to let me know that she would be coming by as well. It was all happening very fast!

There I was still sitting at my kitchen table, sweat now drying on my skin, staring out the window. How little time it took to completely change my life for who knew how long. I thought to myself that I sure hoped that Danielle was ok with us fostering such a young child.

Then it dawned on me how I could get hold of Danielle. I called the sister-in-law of the person Danielle was helping, and asked her to call her brother-in-law to ask Danielle to call me. Danielle called a few minutes later to hear me break the news that we would have an eight-month-old boy in our home by the time she got here. Thankfully, she was very excited. Oh, how our world was about to get rocked!!

Soon, I heard a knock at the front door. I opened it to see a young woman holding a baby boy. He was wide eyed as he looked at me. She introduced herself as I welcomed them in. She handed me the baby while she returned to her car to get his belongings. He did not come with very much. She grabbed a diaper bag with a few items in it. She also brought in a few clothes that she had retrieved from a clothes closet at a CPS office. Some of the clothes were not even the correct size.

I carried the boy into our living room and sat on the floor with him. He was not crying. He did not even seem afraid. I think he was a little bit in shock. The CPS caseworker joined us in the living room and sat on a couch. She seemed nervous, or stressed, or maybe she was rushed. Her cell phone rang several times over the next few minutes. We exchanged small talk as we waited for the Arrow caseworker and Danielle to arrive. Any concern that I originally had for accepting a placement for such a young child was beginning to melt away as I watched him explore his new surroundings. The CPS caseworker began to relax, but her phone kept ringing. She finally turned it off.

After about 20 minutes, Danielle showed up with a huge smile on her face. She was so excited to see the boy on the floor crawling around me. She picked him up and hugged him. He seemed instantly comfortable in her arms. Danielle introduced herself to the CPS caseworker. Then, I let her know that we were waiting on the Arrow caseworker to show up. She showed up a few minutes later. I had never met her before either.

I did not expect to find out much about the boy's case, especially the reason he was being removed, but the Arrow caseworker began asking the CPS caseworker questions almost as soon as she arrived. She would ask a question and then exclaim, "He is sooo cute!", then fire off another question. I began to feel the weight of the situation press down on me as I listened to the two caseworkers talk. To them, it seemed like just another case in the world of foster care. To me, it was the center of the universe at that moment. I sat listening with surprise at how much information they shared in front of us. I did not think that we would ever know much about the case or the family. I thought that we might not even ever meet the family. I apparently was very naive to think that. As I listened, I felt my heart go out to this young child, hearing how he had been injured and neglected.

The CPS caseworker then stated that we needed to get started on the paperwork. I remembered that we were going to be filling out a stack of paperwork, and that was why the CPS caseworker was just sitting there waiting.

To protect the little boy's identity, from now on I will refer to him as Chandler. Chandler is the name of the friend that Danielle was helping at the grocery store at the time I received the call for the placement. Our friend Chandler passed away a few months later after a lengthy battle with cancer. As a way to honor him, I asked his brother for permission to use his name.

At the time, our new foster son seemed very calm as he was observing his new surroundings. I thought that this was odd. I mean, he was just taken from day-care by some stranger and then dropped off at some other stranger's home. I really expected to see a very upset and crying baby. Instead, he was playing with some keys and crawling around looking at things.

We transitioned to the kitchen table to dive into the mountain of paperwork that needed to be filled out and signed. A duplicate of each document had to be signed. One copy was for CPS. One copy was for Arrow. That process drove home the responsibility of what we were agreeing to do.

After a couple hours of hearing Chandler's story and filling out the mound of paperwork, the caseworkers finally left around 6 p.m. Suddenly, we were alone with an eight-month-old boy in our home, and we were now his primary caretakers. As I previously mentioned, all we had was the portable Pack and Play that our friends had loaned us. Thankfully we at least had a place for him to sleep. It was kind of like coming home from the hospital with a newborn that for some strange reason you were not expecting.

Like most new parents, we had no idea what we were doing. The difference with Chandler was that he was already eight-months-old. We did not know what he ate or even the last time he had eaten. We did not know what time he usually went to bed, what his bedtime ritual was, or what he slept in. Because of his age, we knew that CPS required that he not have anything in his crib, including a blanket.

We had no idea how long he would be with us, but I already knew that I would allow him into my heart regardless of the outcome. That simultaneously excited and frightened me, but the decision had been made. Any change of mind on our part would only add to the trauma already in Chandler's life, and he definitely did not need any more. I told myself again that I could do anything for a few weeks.

CHAPTER 10

MAJOR ADJUSTMENT

That first night after the caseworkers left, we began to get things ready for Chandler to sleep. We set up the Pack and Play in a bedroom that already had two twin beds in it, so it was a little cramped in the room. Then we read the instructions on how to prepare the formula that the CPS caseworker brought. He had one bottle in his diaper bag that came with him. Even though he had not been fussing, I was guessing that he had to be hungry. I don't remember what time we put him in bed or if he went right to sleep, but I don't think he cried at all. I would have thought that he would be very scared, but I really do think he was simply in shock.

I cannot imagine what was going on inside the mind of an eight-month-old baby who was experiencing the kind of day he had just had. After I got to know his personality a little better, I could see how he was observing his new environment that first night. He had never met Danielle, the CPS caseworker, the Arrow caseworker, or me before. He had never been in our house before that night. The only real sign of fear that I saw from him was his reaction when he was away from Danielle. It was amazing to me how he seemed immediately attached to her. Almost as soon as she walked into the house, he wanted her to hold him. He would cry if she were out of sight, but as long as she was close by or holding him, Chandler seemed to feel safe.

Danielle and I finally went to bed around 11 p.m. but neither of us could sleep, each of us lost in our own thoughts. I lay there staring at the ceiling, thinking about what had just changed in our family. If you would have asked me a year earlier what our future was going to look like, I would have confidently said that we were going to be on the foreign mission field. Even though we had spent the past year getting certified to foster, we had not made any commitments to a child until this day.

I learned later that Danielle had lain in bed awake for hours, playing over and over in her mind what had happened to Chandler. She hardly slept at all that first night. She immediately became the protective mother. It was hard for either of us to understand why or how someone could injure a child, especially their own.

A little after midnight, a loud thunderstorm rolled through. I was surprised that Chandler slept through it. If he did wake up, he did not make any noise. I had not fallen asleep yet. I lay there thinking about his young mother. I wondered if she also was listening to the storm wondering where her son was. I know that I would have been! Did she wonder if he was safe or scared? I could not imagine the pain, anger, and confusion, and countless other possible emotions Chandler's family must have been feeling that night.

I am glad that we were committed to fostering, because the first several days after Chandler was placed in our home were intense. Trying to adjust to having an eight-month-old boy in our home was extremely overwhelming. It really was like bringing home a newborn except we had not made any preparations at all for him. I was a bundle of emotions. I was confused and frustrated about how no one in his extended family seemed willing to step forward to care for him. Yet, I was filled with joy that we had a child in our home. I was also apprehensive and cautious about my ability to care for such a young child.

Before Chandler came into our lives, our normal time to go to bed was around 11 p.m., and we were used to getting up around 7 a.m. That quickly changed! Chandler was waking up around 5 a.m., and during the day he was taking very short naps. We did not know if this was what Chandler's normal sleep patterns had been like, but I think a lot of it had to do with him not feeling safe. We really knew very little about this baby boy. Obviously, this was a huge adjustment for us. For the first couple weeks or so, Danielle was going to bed soon after Chandler did each night, and we were taking turns getting up with him during the night. After a couple weeks of this, we were beginning to wear down. I told myself again that we could do anything for a few weeks. It turns out that those first couple weeks were going to test my resolve.

I shared about how Chandler had an ear infection within a week of him living with us. It was also the same night that we had some out-of-town guests spend a couple nights with us. About a week later, I had my 50th birthday party. What a way to celebrate the big 5-0! What was I thinking, getting an eight-month-old baby boy for my 50th? Then I got a painful sinus infection that put me out of commission for a couple days, leaving Danielle to take care of Chandler by herself. On top of that, Danielle's car broke down the first time she took Chandler to the grocery store. I was beginning to wonder how much more was going to be piled on. Was this a test of our commitment? No wonder we were completely exhausted after a couple weeks.

I really thought that Chandler was going to live with us for a few weeks at most. At least that was the impression I got from the caseworkers. They kept telling us that someone in Chandler's extended family was going to get custody of him. That thought kept me going through the sleepless nights and long days. Don't get me wrong—I enjoyed him living with us. However, I still was not sure if I was prepared to raise such a young child.

After about six weeks, which flew by in a blur, we were finally getting into a better routine. About the only area of struggle was his sleeping. If he napped for 45 minutes, that was great! He would take two short naps during the day, which many times were taken as opportunities for Danielle and I to nap, too. We had to rock him to sleep every night. Sometimes that would take more than an hour. I know now that we probably were exacerbating the whole nighttime ritual, but we were doing what we thought was best at the time. We were definitely rookies when it came to caring for a baby, particularly a baby that was experiencing the effects of trauma. When he would scream and wrap his body around me every time I tried to lay him down to sleep, I just did not feel right prying him off, laying him down, and walking out of the room. So I would rock him until he was completely asleep.

One night, Danielle went out to dinner with a friend while I kept Chandler. I began trying to put him to bed for the night around 7 p.m.

When Danielle got home at 9 p.m., I was still trying to get him to go to sleep. Every time I thought he was asleep, I would try to lay him gently in his bed. As soon as I let go of him, he would begin screaming. Man, was I frustrated! I felt like screaming right along with him. I have no doubt that Danielle could tell by my expression as soon as she walked in that it had been a rough time. We had a few more nights like that for a while. Many nights we took turns sleeping in his room. If we were there when he woke up, then he seemed to go back to sleep quickly.

Before you criticize our parenting, remember that we had never had children of our own. We did not know how much our parenting inexperience versus the trauma of being removed from his family affected his sleeplessness. We tried anything to help Chandler adjust to his new surroundings and feel safe. My mindset was probably a little different than a typical new parent. At the time, I saw us as Chandler's safe place, his stability, and his refuge. So if that meant a little discomfort for me, then so be it.

The weeks turned into months. Around the middle of August 2011, our CPS caseworker told us that Chandler would probably remain with us at least until December. When December came, she told us that he would be with us until March 2012. Well, March came and went, and Chandler was still with us.

As the time Chandler lived with us loomed on, we had more adjustments to make than just sleeping patterns. Danielle and I could no longer make spontaneous decisions to go somewhere. It took much longer to get out the door with a young child in our family. Sometimes we arranged for babysitters days in advance, which is not easy for foster children. After 20 plus years of not ever having to arrange for childcare, this was a major adjustment for us.

We were not only logistically prepared for older foster children, for example twin beds in the bedroom, but we also had to adjust mentally to having a baby in our home.

I love it when I am able to see how God has been working in my life preparing me for something. This was one of those occasions. For about three years we led a Bible study for young couples with preschoolers. I thought that it was ironic that we taught this class when we did not have any children of our own. We became close to these families. When we shared with them about our decision to foster and possibly adopt they rallied around us. Often they would ask about how our training was going. After we were certified, they eagerly waited with us to find out about a child being placed with us. They prayed with and for us as we prepared to be foster or adoptive parents.

The first night Chandler was with us, Danielle sent an email to the group with the news that Chandler was in our home. The very next day, three of the ladies from the group showed up at our house. All three of them were preschool moms. They came with clothes, toys, baby bottles, diapers, and so on. It was like a surprise baby shower. It just so happened that our new baby weighed 20 pounds, was already crawling, and was eight-months-old! I laugh at the irony of it all. It was as if we were prepared to come home from the hospital with an eight-year-old and instead we came home with an eight-month-old. I am thankful that we were strongly connected to this small group of preschool families. It was God's providence to help meet our needs in this moment. Only God knew back then how those relationships would bless us now that we had a baby living with us.

CHAPTER 11

FAMILY INTERACTION

I f all we had to do was adapt to having a new member of our family who happened to be eight-months-old, that would have been quite an adjustment all by itself. However, it quickly became evident that Chandler's family was going to be a part of the equation.

When we were in our training classes, a common discussion centered around birth parent visits. We all wanted to know what they were like so we could know what to expect. We heard all kinds of stories, some good and some bad. I pictured what these parent visits would look like based on these stories. I envisioned driving up to a CPS office that had a secret door for foster parents only to use when we dropped off our foster child. We would pull up to the door, make the secret knock, and a CPS caseworker would take the child from us. Then we would leave without ever encountering the family. Ha! What kind of fantasy land was I living in? I must not have been listening very closely in class because our first parent visit was nothing like that.

The first visit was scheduled just a couple of days after Chandler was placed with us. It took place in a nondescript office building and was scheduled for one hour supervised by a CPS caseworker. I decided to go with Danielle so that she would not experience this unknown encounter alone. Parent visits are one of the ways that foster parents are expected to help with the reconciliation of the foster child to his family. This means that a foster family has to adjust their schedule to make this happen. Because the foster child's family might live in a different county, the visits can be an hour or more drive. Thankfully, for us, the first several birth parent visits were scheduled at a CPS office not far from our home.

As we drove up to the building, I began looking for the secret door. I drove around the building a couple times without seeing any door marked as the drop-off point. What I did see was a young couple watching us, a couple that fit the description of Chandler's parents. They had just parked and were straining to see in my vehicle. I knew it had to be Chandler's parents. How was I supposed to drop off Chandler without interacting with his family? Reluctantly, I parked on the opposite side of the building, and we all got out.

We walked down a long sidewalk up to some double glass doors. Through the glass doors, I could see the young couple staring earnestly back at us. As they saw Chandler, they definitely now knew who we were. We opened the doors and walked into a sterile waiting room with about four rows of hard plastic chairs, all facing the doors. I felt a small wave of nausea wash over me. I really did not want to meet his parents, at least not on the very first parent visit, but I had no choice now.

Chandler's mother said hello with a smile and reached out for Chandler. Chandler's father shook my hand as though he was unsure if I would bite him. He barely looked at me as he introduced himself. This was not how I had envisioned this going down. I had some concern about how they would react to us. We had heard a few horror stories in which the parents reacted with some anger towards the foster parents, so I was braced for anything.

I was struck by how young they looked. We had been told their approximate ages, but they seemed so much younger to me when I saw them. They could have easily been my own kids in this tough situation. Even though I was reluctant about meeting them, my heart immediately softened toward them. I was a little surprised at how grateful they seemed to be that we were caring for their son. I still had serious reservations about anyone who would injure a child, so I was very guarded in my interactions with them. I wondered where the CPS caseworker was. I needed her to insulate this encounter with the parents.

Soon the caseworker arrived and greeted everyone, apologizing for running a little late. It was an awkward moment as we handed Chandler over to his parents. Then they disappeared down a hall to a room for their one-hour visit. I later learned that the visitation room was a small room with simple furniture and a dirty rug on the floor. There was nothing in the room for the children to read or play with, so it was up to either the biological parents or foster parents to bring something. The caseworker supervised the visit in an adjacent room. The whole environment felt very penal to me, very prison-like. Even though Chandler had been with us for only a few days, it felt strange to let him go without my going with him. I already felt like his protector.

Since the visit was only for one hour, we did not have time to go very far, but I had no interest in sitting in that waiting room. As we left the parking lot, I drove by the couple's car and wrote down their license plate number. I wanted to know it in case they found out where we lived; we might see them driving by. I know I was paranoid, but I had no idea what to expect. Even though I was not worried about them, I was not going to assume that they would not do something foolish. That is why we did not tell them our last names when we met them. I was even a little concerned that they had seen what I drove that day.

We decided to go to a nearby grocery store to pick up some baby supplies that we sorely needed now that we had a baby boy living with us. On our drive to the grocery store, Danielle and I processed what had just transpired at the CPS office. We both agreed that we needed to be careful about how much information we gave the young parents. We made our way to the baby aisles and began looking at all of the stuff for babies. I wanted to buy him everything that I saw in the store for a child his age! After staring at baby food, baby formula, bottles, pacifiers, toys, and so on, I began to feel disoriented and dizzy. I had felt this way a few times before. When we first moved to Thailand, I felt this way; I also felt this way a few weeks after we moved back to the U.S. I was experiencing culture shock. One day we had no children in our home, and the next day I was in a grocery store buying baby supplies. We filled our grocery basket with jars of baby food, cans of baby formula, and other necessities.

We went back to the CPS office a little early to make sure that no one had to wait on us to pick up Chandler. We were standing in the waiting room when the parents emerged from the hallway with Chandler in his mother's arms. Chandler did not seem sad or happy. I think he was still in a state of shock, maybe trying to understand what was going on.

His young parents again expressed their gratefulness for us caring for Chandler. I found that odd, but I was thankful that they were not angry toward us. Then Chandler's mother began asking a lot of questions that made Danielle and me very uncomfortable. There was nothing wrong with her questions. I just was not expecting them. In fact, if I were in her shoes, I would ask questions too. She wanted to know if we had kids of our own and if had we fostered any other children. I think that she was nervous, insecure, and possibly ashamed for what was happening. She seemed to have the kind of personality that probably talks a lot when she gets nervous. Chandler's father, however, was very quiet. Sometimes it is the quiet ones who make me more nervous.

As much as I felt bad for her, I did not want to be naive and overly trusting. My nature is to believe that people have good intentions, but I have learned over the years that such is not always the case. Because we had been entrusted to care for Chandler, I was skeptical about why she was asking so many questions. Someone in this family had injured and neglected Chandler, and I knew that he was safe with us. It was time for us to leave, so they awkwardly handed Chandler back to us. I once again was surprised that Chandler showed no emotion as his mother handed him to Danielle.

We all walked out of the building together. I was thankful I had parked on the opposite side. Looking back now, I know that Chandler must have still been in shock from all what was happening to him. A child his age in normal circumstances would have been upset to be leaving his mother again. As we walked back to our vehicle, I remember him watching his parents walk away in the other direction with a blank, nonchalant expression. That scene broke my heart.

On the drive home, I drove like I was in a spy movie. I kept checking my mirrors to see if their car was following us. I would slow down to let cars pass me, and I took a circuitous route back to our house. I am laughing at myself as I am writing this. What a paranoid goofball! But I truly wanted to make sure that they were not going to follow us home and confront us.

For the first few nights after the parent visit, I continued to make sure that I was not being followed home, always closed my garage door, and even asked my neighbor across the street to let me know if he saw anyone suspicious around our house. Even though Chandler's family had not shown any aggressive behavior towards us, I did not want to take any chances. It felt strange to me to have a baby boy in our home who had been taken away from another family. It would not have surprised us if they had done some Internet research to find out who we were and where we lived. If I had been in their shoes, I would want to know who my child was living with and that he was safe. Looking back on those first encounters with Chandler's family, I can see now that God was granting us favor with them.

The parent visits turned out to be one of the hardest adjustments not only for Danielle and me, but also for Chandler. When we got home after that first parent visit, Chandler took one of his toys and began to bang it against his head while crying. It was heartbreaking to see such a young child reacting in this way. Even though none of his behaviors after that was as extreme, he still struggled after each parent visit. We began to see a pattern each week. Chandler would begin crying and clinging to Danielle whenever she walked into the CPS office with him. He would cry as Danielle handed him over for his visit. When Chandler would see Danielle after the visit, he seemed happy to be reuniting with her. Then for about two days after his parent visit, Chandler would have a couple of sleepless nights, be more defiant and fussy, and was definitely more clingy. Eventually, we learned what to expect, and sadly, this became the norm for a while.

My unrealistic expectation of never having to interact with the parents was quickly corrected. I also found out very early on that not only were we going to meet the parents, but we were also going to encounter several others in the family.

The week after Chandler was placed with us, a court hearing was scheduled to authorize the permanency plan. For some reason, the hearing kept getting postponed. I had no interest in attending the hearing anyway. If Chandler was going to be with us for just a few days or weeks as originally projected, I did not see any reason to meet more of the family. I wanted to remain as emotionally unattached from the case as possible. The delay in the court hearing prolonged the court's authorization of Chandler's custody plan. What we understood from our caseworker was that CPS was looking for other family members to take temporary custody of Chandler, which apparently is the normal course of action. This is one of the reasons that we thought he would be with us for only a few days or a couple weeks at most.

Finally, the court hearing was reset. Then our CPS caseworker informed us of a family meeting scheduled at the CPS office a few days before the hearing. Both our CPS and Arrow caseworker encouraged us to attend the meeting. They asked us to bring Chandler, too. The meeting informed all parties of the permanency plan for the biological family. CPS develops a permanency plan for all biological families with the primary goal of reunification. The CPS caseworker wanted the parents and extended family to see Chandler. I think they also wanted to see how the family interacted with him. I began to understand that I had an unrealistic picture of what fostering was like. Apparently I was naive enough to think that all that I was responsible for was taking care of a child. As it turned out, we met several of the extended family members, and we also found out a lot more about Chandler's case than we cared to know.

On the day of the meeting, we showed up at the same drab CPS office where Chandler had had his first parent visit. Again, we slowly walked down the sidewalk toward the front doors. As we approached the door, I could see several people standing around inside. When they saw us, their faces lit up with big smiles, and a woman not much older than I reached out for Chandler. She turned out to be his paternal grandmother. I handed Chandler over to her, and he seemed happy and comfortable with her. I felt a blend of emotions wash over me. I was glad to see that there were family members who loved this child, but I was also concerned about what had happened to cause CPS to be involved. I also felt a little twinge of sadness. I was enjoying being this child's foster dad, but this scene reinforced the fact that he was not my son. How could I so quickly become attached to him?

I looked around the room to see who else was there. Chandler's mother and father were there, along with Chandler's maternal grandfather and two lawyers. One lawyer represented the father and the other represented the mother. The scene reminded me of an awkward family reunion that you go to at which you see people to whom you think you are related, but since you have not seen them in awhile, you are not even sure what their names are. The tension in this room had that same feel.

After a few moments of waiting and watching the family pass Chandler around, the CPS caseworkers ushered us into a conference room just off the waiting room. Four tables had been pushed together to make one large table with chairs all the way around. In addition to Chandler's family and us, the meeting included three CPS employees, a facilitator, Chandler's CPS caseworker, and a supervisor. Our caseworker from Arrow was also in attendance. Understandably, tension filled the air. I was surprised when Chandler's mom handed him back to me as we all took seats around the table. I thought that the family would want to hold him as long as possible. The CPS staff sat at one end of the table. Danielle led us to seats next to them, while I held Chandler. The family and their lawyers took seats at the other end of the table. I was still wondering why the caseworker wanted us to bring an eight-month-old baby to this meeting with such intense emotions right under the surface.

We soon learned that the paternal grandmother had found out about Chandler's placement in foster care just a few days before this meeting. Apparently, she was not very involved in his life at that time. She was undeniably upset by the fact that she had not been contacted. That spoke volumes to me about the family dynamics.

The CPS caseworker began explaining the permanency plan to the family. There were two plans. The first plan was reconciliation with one or both of the parents. They were not married but were still dating. The second plan was adoption by someone in the extended family. The parents were informed of several steps that they needed to complete over a six-month period in order for them to get Chandler back. I learned that this was a very common plan for families involved with CPS. If one or both of the parents would simply work through the plan laid out for them by CPS, they could get their son back within a few months. In the meantime, I thought that surely someone else in the family would want to and would be able to take custody of Chandler. The goal of the meeting was for everyone involved to understand the plan. At the same time, CPS was actively pursuing a possible temporary placement with a family member. Again, I really thought that Chandler would be with us for just a few more days. Obviously the extended family members in that room seemed interested in and cared for Chandler.

As the meeting went on, the tension in the room found its way to the middle of my shoulders and worked its way up the back of my neck and into my head. By the time the meeting was over, I had a pounding headache. Neither Danielle nor I said anything during the meeting. We just listened, observed, and kept Chandler occupied as much as possible. At the end of the meeting, a sheet was passed around for us to sign showing that we were in attendance. How were we going to sign without the family learning our last names? I still felt paranoid that they would try to find out where we lived. Danielle signed first and just put her first name. So I did the same. I could not help but wonder what we had gotten ourselves into.

After the meeting, everyone slowly made their way out of the room. Different family members took turns holding Chandler as we walked back to the waiting area. Everyone in the family at some level expressed their appreciation to us for caring for Chandler. The whole thing seemed so surreal. Most of the family members had expressed their displeasure with CPS in the family meeting, but their interactions with us were pleasant. The CPS caseworker hung around for a few minutes before she nudged us out the door. It was a stark reminder that they were in charge and that no one in the family was to have time with Chandler without supervision by someone from CPS. I left there that day understanding that we were going to know more about the family and Chandler's case than I originally had wanted. What was not clear to me was how long Chandler would be in our lives.

During those first few weeks when it seemed like Chandler would be moved to a family member's home at any time, I knew that I was guarding my heart. It was tough because I immediately felt attached to him because of the traumatic situation that he was in. I automatically felt a need to protect him. Not to mention he was a cute little boy!

The problem with me trying to guard my heart was that the longer it took for them to decide where to place him, the more I began to feel like a low-paid, unappreciated baby sitter. I think it is hard to watch someone else's child for a long period of time. I needed to begin thinking of Chandler as my own son regardless of how long he was going to live with us. Otherwise, I was going to be on an emotional roller coaster and begin to resent everyone involved. I knew that by thinking of Chandler as my own son, I would essentially let him into my heart, but I had to do this so that I would not harbor any resentment. I knew he was not my son, and some days I was fully reminded of this, especially when he had parent visits. However, when I would walk into his room at night to watch him sleep, I felt that I was watching my son. I began to love him as my son. I disciplined him as my own son. I taught him things as if he were my son. And if the day came when he left our home, I knew it would feel like I was losing my son. I began praying for God's grace for that day if it were to come.

God showed me that he had been fostering in me the heart of a father. I saw that I was not as selfish as I thought I was. I found out that I had a heart that desired the best for this child over my own wants or needs.

CHAPTER 12

COURT HEARINGS

Purpose of Court Hearings

Some may refer to court hearings as status hearings. That is what most of them really are. The initial hearing is for the purpose of filing the permanency plan, which in most cases is family reunification. Subsequent hearings, which are typically every six months, check on the progress of that plan. If the biological parents are following the plan, the hearings begin to discuss the reunification plan. If the parents are not complying with the requirements set forth by the court, the hearings move in a couple of different directions. The court might agree to place the child in the custody of an extended family member, either temporarily or permanently. Or, the court might decide to terminate the parental rights. If this happens, the hopeful outcome for the child is adoption by another family. If the child is adopted, the state is no longer involved in his life. If the child is not adopted, then the court continues to hold status hearings for the child for as long as he or she remains in foster care.

My Experience

Since I did not want to know much about the case or even to meet the family, I certainly did not plan to go to the court hearings. I did not attend the first hearing, which was held in June 2011. I learned later that the case did not even go before the judge. All the attorneys and caseworkers met in the hall to discuss the permanency plan. Since all parties agreed to the plan, they all signed off on it. However, by the time of the second hearing, Chandler had lived with us for several months, I knew a lot about his case, and I met several of the family members. I was invested. I now wanted to attend the court hearings.

I really did not know what to expect at a court hearing, and it was a little bit intimidating. It had been a few years since I had been in a courtroom, so I had forgotten about dockets. When I was told that the case was at 9 a.m., I rushed to get there on time. I did not see anyone that I recognized, which made me wonder if I had the right courtroom. I walked in and out of the courtroom a few times, and down the massive hall to another courtroom. Finally, I saw an agenda on the wall outside the first courtroom. I read down the docket and saw Chandler's parent's names listed. I still did not see anyone that I knew was associated with the case, but I went on in and quietly found a seat.

I quickly surmised that I had underdressed. I wore a nice shirt, a pair of jeans, and boots. Most were more nicely dressed than I. The bailiff asked one gentlemen to tuck in his shirt, and asked another women to throw away her chewing gum, so there was a definite protocol to follow. The judge, attorneys, caseworkers, bailiffs, and the other regulars all knew their roles, but I did not know mine. The inside of the courtroom looked like what I expected. Just inside the doors were a few rows of chairs and benches. A short wall separated the seats from where all the arguments and decisions took place. To the left of the judge's bench was a jury box. Inside the short wall was a long desk where the county attorneys busily looked over the day's docket. To the right of the judge's bench was the witness stand.

Attorneys of all kind were scurrying about, conferring with their clients, negotiating deals with other attorneys, or getting the cases lined up and ready for the judge. Some caseworkers typed away on reports on their laptops, trying to get caught up on their mountains of paperwork as they waited for the cases to begin. Other caseworkers whispered quietly among themselves or with families attending the hearing. The bailiff leaned on a piece of furniture, glancing about the courtroom. I found the different characters in this real life drama intriguing. Some looked very professional. Others looked as if they had stayed out too late the night before and could not find anything in their closet that was not wrinkled. Then, there were the clients, some with their families. Most of them looked anxious about what was about to happen. It was like a scene from one of the courtroom drama series that I have watched over the years.

Finally, our CPS caseworker, Arrow caseworker, and attorneys working on the case began to show up. Our Arrow caseworker came and sat by me. She had another case down the hall, so she shuttled back and forth between the two courtrooms. I saw members of Chandler's family enter the courtroom and sit on the other side from me. We waved at one another, but we did not talk to each other until after the case was heard.

I sat for more than two hours before Chandler's case was heard, but I found the activity in the room interesting. I noticed that our CPS caseworker spent quite a bit of time in the hallway conversing with Chandler's family.

Finally, Chandler's case was called and all the parties, except our Arrow caseworker and me as the foster parent, made their way up to the front. The county attorney, CPS caseworker, the attorney for Chandler's mother, the attorney for his father, Chandler's father, and Chandler's *ad litem* (an attorney appointed to act on behalf of a child) all stood facing the judge. It proceeded like an interview conducted by the county attorney while the judge listened. Questions ranged from the well-being of Chandler, the state of his current living conditions and relationship with his caretakers, to how Chandler's parents were doing with the plan that CPS required of them for reunification with Chandler.

I am not sure how all the attorneys, judges, caseworkers, and the other court employees dealt with the depressing stories that unfolded in the courtroom day after day—stories about marriages ending in divorce, battles over the custody of children, children removed from abusive homes, parental rights being terminated. Occasionally, there were hopeful stories about parents working hard so that their children were returned. Sometimes, there were uplifting stories about a child adopted into a loving family. But for the most part, the stories were about brokenness.

I ended up attending three more court hearings in Chandler's case, March, June, and September 2012. The last three hearings were only three months apart. By the September hearing, I knew the routine, and I was getting to know the attorneys and caseworkers better. I concluded that it is important for a foster parent to attend the court hearings if at all possible. I think that it communicates that the foster child is in good hands. Sure, the hearings are boring after a while, but I learned a lot about Chandler's case by attending. I even had a few positive interactions with Chandler's family. I also think that it was comforting to them that Chandler's case was important enough for me to attend.

The March 2012 hearing was much like the December 2011 hearing. But the June and September 2012 hearings were much different. You will have to wait and read about them later!

LESSONS LEARNED

CHAPTER 13

STAY IN THE MOMENT

The only way I knew how to love Chandler as my own son, knowing that if he left our family some day my heart would break, was to stay in the moment. What I mean is that I had to stay focused on that day, that moment even. If I began to worry about what might happen in the future, I could not fully love Chandler in the present. A friend of mine related to me some advice he received along these lines. The advice was to avoid four words that rob of us from being able to stay in the moment: "what if" and "if only." I knew that I did not have the luxury of thinking these thoughts if I was going to be able to make the most of the time that I was being granted to spend with Chandler. God put me in situations for several years teaching me how to do just that. I am not always a good student.

Growing up, I was insecure, unsure of myself, and was a people-pleaser. As I got older, I had accumulated a list of regrets, and I was afraid and uncertain about what the future held for me. I became very good at hiding this from others. Most people would probably guess that I was confident and knew what I wanted to do with my life. To protect my real self, I would simply keep people at a distance. Sadly, even those who considered themselves my close friends really did not know me. After awhile, I hardly knew myself.

I can remember as a young teenager daydreaming about what it would be like to be someone else. I never dreamed I was a famous person. Rather, I dreamed I was some of my peers, just kids I knew from school. Having that kind of personality made it nearly impossible to know how to live in the present. I was either trying to figure out how to undo my past or living in fear of my future. God had a big project on His hands with me. It was not until I was in my late 30s that I began to understand my dilemma. I knew that I struggled with anxiety, trying to please others, and the destructive lifestyle that ensues. I did not understand how to be at peace with myself, to truly understand whom I was in Christ, and to live in the moment. God has graciously taught me that staying or living in the moment is part of what He is talking about in John 15. He calls it abiding or resting in Him. A counselor, who became a friend, helped me understand how living with regret about the past or in fear of the future only robs us of our ability to live in the moment. The result is not living in reality. I did not like experiencing pain, any kind of pain—physical, emotional, or relational. I did whatever it took to avoid it. By God's grace, He has been revealing truth to me, and as a result, He has brought healing to me in this area. I still struggle with this issue, but at least I am usually aware of it. .

A great example of how God redeemed my brokenness in this area is when we moved to Thailand in 2007 for six months. I quit my job of 11 years so we could volunteer as missionaries. In my corporate career, I was focused short-term on a project that I had been working on for nearly a year. Long-term, I was in the process of obtaining some certification in the field of project management. When Danielle and I decided to take this step of faith, I was not sure if I would return to my place of employment or that career path when we moved back home. I was hoping that I could take a six-month leave of absence and then come back to my old job. I was informed that I could not do that, so I resigned. I did not know if they would re-hire me when I returned. If not, I had no idea at the time what I would be doing. However I definitely had felt God calling us to make this change.

We moved to Thailand, trusting that God would take care of us when we returned. It would have been natural and easy for me to be worried about employment when I returned. I could have easily spent time in Thailand making sure I had a job waiting for me when I got back home. In the past, I would have spent time fretting over the decision I had made and worrying about what was going to happen in the future. Instead, I decided to embrace the time that I had in Thailand.

The six months that we lived in Thailand were a total life-changing event for me. Whether we return to the mission field long-term or not, those months in Thailand transformed me forever. Because I was not spending my free time worried about what was going to happen after the six months were over, I volunteered with several ministries, engaged the local culture, and developed deep relationships. When it was time to leave, it was one of the most difficult days in my life, partly because I was fully invested in every relationship that I had made and in each day while we lived there.

Before I left, I asked God to give me some inkling of an idea about what I would be doing after my return home at least by the time I was on the plane flying back. He answered that prayer. About one month before our scheduled return, I began to talk with a couple of leaders in our home church. Some changes in the staff were taking shape while I was gone. A position for a part-time mission pastor had opened up. I eventually agreed to a temporary, part-time position that gave me the flexibility to leave at any time if Danielle and I decided to return to the mission field full-time. Not only did this answer my request of knowing what I would be doing when I returned home, but it also met a need that the church had. When I had quit my job and left for Thailand a few months earlier, I had no idea that this opportunity would be available. I am learning that when I trust God with my future and focus on staying in the moment, He is more than capable of providing for my every need.

Fostering children has given God a whole new level of opportunity to teach me how to stay in the moment. We had no way of knowing how long Chandler would be with us. I could have spent time wondering if I had made the right decision to become licensed to foster instead of going overseas to be a missionary. I could have fretted over how I had thrown away my corporate career and wondered if it was too late to return to that path. I could worry about what tomorrow held. I could focus on what the future with or without Chandler might look like. When would he leave? Who would end up taking him? Would they take good care of him? Would Chandler be upset? Would he understand what was happening? Would he miss us? Would he recover? People around us asked us about his future all the time. They meant no harm, but it did not do me any good. I tried to be gracious in my responses, but inside I was screaming, "He is with us now. Today I am his dad!"

Dwelling on what the future may hold only creates anxiety for me, and like I shared before, I don't deal with anxiety very well. I become depressed, irritable, or try to escape the emotion. It does not affect just me, but everyone close to me. It definitely affects my wife. She has to put up with my sharp tongue or my moping around the house with a long, sad face. I am pathetic when I get anxious about things, and I saw it affect Chandler, too. Even though he was not talking when he came to us, he easily picked up on my emotions. If I was unsettled, he was unsettled. If I was calm, then even if he was having a bad day, he tended to calm down more easily. He had already had a traumatic enough life. I did not need to add to it just because I could not deal with what the future might look like.

By staying in the moment, I was able to see that what I was doing had great importance. I did not compare it to "greater things" that I could be doing. In that moment, being Chandler's foster daddy was the most important thing in the world. Sometimes when I spent several hours taking care of him or changing multiple dirty diapers, I wondered if I was wasting my time. I struggled with this early on. I remember walking into the living room one day while Chandler was taking a nap and declaring to my wife, "I am wasting my life! I need to find something to do that is more productive!" What I was really saying is that I needed to be doing something that I thought other people would think was more important. At the very least, I felt I needed to be doing something that seemed more important to *me*. Then I would remember that for this little boy, that very moment was the most important time in his young life. Not knowing what his future held, I needed to grab hold of each moment he was in my life, both for him and for me.

When I accepted the importance of this reality, it gave me patience, focus, and the desire to intentionally pray for Chandler. How much more joy would I have if I could apply this truth to all areas of my life? I know that I have to give up some things in order to live this way, like being concerned about what others think, regretting past decisions, being obsessed about what tomorrow holds, and holding too tightly to my personal daily agenda. It seems necessary to put some thought into what lies ahead and to plan for it, but not to the point that I cannot live fully in the present moment. It is also important to remember the past to learn from our experiences and mistakes, but I do not want that to prevent me from experiencing and learning from what life has in store for me today, in this very moment.

The temporary nature of fathering Chandler was imminent. I told myself that even if Chandler somehow ended up with us, the urgency remained. The fact that I am nearly 50 years older than Chandler caused me to have this sense of urgency. When he is 20, I will be almost 70, God willing. I knew that if we experienced the joy of adopting Chandler, I wanted to continue living in the moment each day with an eye on his future. I wanted him to know, love, and trust God, know how to love others well, how to handle money wisely, and live life with confidence.

Parenting with urgency is important for any parent. I have heard parents of grown children often comment how the time flies by, so they implore young parents to take hold of the time that they have with their children while they are still at home. When we are in our 20's and 30's, the thought of our children living with us for 18 to 20 years seems like an eternity. Then we look up and we are in our 40's or 50's and our children are leaving home. Parents think back and wonder if they have done a good enough job, or regret the opportunities they missed to instill better qualities or simply to spend time together. Being a foster dad is a microcosm of this. I was constantly reminded that my son would probably be with me for a very brief time. Staying in the moment affected how I spent my time each day with him. I tried not to put off until the next day things I could do with him on that day. I played on the floor a lot with cars, blocks, stuffed animals, and books that have more pictures than words. I played the same games and watched the same things over and over and over. I got slobbered on and coughed on and sometimes peed on.

We could have been fostering a child who was five, ten, or fifteen years old. I hope that I still would have entered their world regardless of their age, living for that day and cherishing each moment. I would hope that this investment would have a great impact on their future.

We all only have a short window of time to invest in our children regardless if they are our biological, foster, or adopted children. Their destiny is worth it. How much sweeter the time is if we can stay in the moment.

CHAPTER 14

SUPPORT AND ENCOURAGEMENT

Logistical Support

I have always had a tendency to do things on my own. If someone would ask me if I wanted or needed help, I nearly always declined the offer, thank you very much. Thankfully, God had been already working on changing this in my life because we needed support and encouragement.

I am not downplaying the fact that parents of biological children also need support. However, foster parents are almost always dealing with traumatized children. Foster children, no matter what their age, have experienced trauma that a biological child hopefully has not had to endure. Being removed from one's family is traumatic enough, but in order for a child to be removed, there was some kind of physical or sexual abuse, abandonment, or neglect. Any person would have difficulty processing these things. How much harder it must be for a child, especially a young one who does not have the ability to communicate what he is feeling and thinking. Caring for a child who has experienced and continues to experience trauma can be very challenging. Providing an informed, caring support structure around foster families is vital.

Some of the support is simple logistics. We received calls about potential foster children that ranged in age from eight months to 12 years old. It would not make sense for us to try to have all the basics on hand for all of these ages. We were more prepared for an older child, so when Chandler was placed with us as an eight-month-old, we needed almost everything for a baby. That is why it meant so much to us when our friends showed up with all the baby items the day after Chandler was placed in our home. It would have taken us a lot of time and effort to get all the things that we needed. Since we did not know how long he would be with us, having baby items loaned to us was a huge support.

Sometimes the support comes in the form of babysitting. Parents of toddlers always appreciate a break to go out to dinner or to a movie or simply to run errands. We were no different. A big difference, though, is that foster parents cannot have just anyone watch their foster children. The state has requirements for anyone who babysits a foster child. These requirements quickly narrow the babysitter pool available for foster parents. Even though we never felt a need to take a long break of several days away from Chandler, we did try to get out for a date from time to time. We enlisted the help of a friend who already met most of the requirements, and we recruited a few others as well. We also swapped babysitting with some other foster parents. This simple act of babysitting provided much needed support when we needed a break. If we decide to not have another long-term foster placement, I will strongly consider babysitting for other foster families.

Emotional Support

Another need that foster parents have is emotional support and encouragement. Many friends and family took the time to visit us, hang out, pray, and love on Chandler and us. Even brief, simple words of encouragement strengthened us when it was most needed.

I especially appreciated the way both of our families supported us in our decision to open our home to foster children, even though some kept their distance from Chandler in order to protect their hearts. Other family members loved on Chandler just as if he was a permanent part of our family. Danielle's mother especially became very attached to Chandler, so much so that sometimes she peppered us with questions about Chandler's future. At the time, we had no idea what was going happen with Chandler. We trusted God with his future. She asked a few times if we would stay in touch with Chandler if he went back to his family. We most likely would not stay in touch. I did not want to cause his transition back to his family to be harder than it needed to be. My prayer was that if he was only with us a few months that they would be positive ones that provided him a solid foundation. When I explained this to Danielle's mom, she put on a pouty face and then asked me if *she* could stay in touch with Chandler! I had to laugh because when we first began talking about adopting through the foster system, she was not very supportive. God has a way of opening up our hearts to those who need His love. It is a source of joy when we are a vessel of His love.

Danielle has also found support in befriending other moms of preschoolers. For obvious reasons, a lot of preschool moms seek each other out for support. A common activity is to have play dates. It gives the kids an opportunity to play with other children and get some of their energy out, and it gives the moms time for grown-up talk. Even though most of these moms are in their 20's and 30's, Danielle enjoys hanging out with them. They are also good resources to learn ways to care for and raise a toddler. Danielle and Chandler are both very social and love being around other people, so these play dates are a joy for both of them.

Networks of Support

A growing network of families, churches, and agencies provide support for those who are fostering and adopting. Seminars and conferences are offered throughout the year, giving foster and adoptive families great information. In order to retain our license, Arrow requires us to have 30 hours of continuing education each year per person. Even though I rarely look forward to sitting through a class or conference, I nearly always benefit greatly from them. Over the past 10-20 years, more and more books and online resources have also become available to help families raising foster children. I think all of these resources will continue to grow as the faith community as a whole continues to respond to caring for at-risk children.

Even though God's Word has a very clear call to care for orphans, not everyone fosters or adopts. Many others are needed to care for them in supportive ways. I know that I am thankful for the support we have received. Remember, instead of focusing on the enormity of the need for foster and adoptive homes, let God direct you to the life of one or two at-risk children and ask how He might want you to care for them. I promise that it won't be hard to find a child who needs you. Yes, it will cost you something, maybe even some heartache, but I also promise you that you will be blessed by being obedient to God's call.

CHAPTER 15

MORE THAN ONE CHILD

I once attended a conference about orphan care. I went to a breakout session about ways the local Western church can impact the worldwide orphan crisis. A statement was made that has continued to resonate with me: one of the largest unreached people groups in the world are the orphans found in every country.

In missiological circles, the term "people group" is used a lot. In a broad sense, the term refers to a group of people that have something that binds them together, such as a common language, culture, location, caste, tradition, history, and so on. The statement stretched the definition of people groups a little bit, but the point hit home with me.

If we really want to reach every nation, tribe, and people group, a powerful way is for the church to reach out to those who have been orphaned. These are children who are vulnerable, at-risk, and impressionable. They are crying out for someone to love them unconditionally. If we as the church do not step into this void, then the void will continue to be filled by Satan, damning another generation. These children do not exist in a vacuum. Satan, the enemy, is filling the void with abuse, human trafficking, neglect, and hopelessness.

We need to wake up and be who God is calling us to be. We need to push back this injustice that has thrived for generations. It has not gotten any better in our time. In fact, it may be worse. Thankfully, some well-known organizations, such as Compassion International, World Vision, and others are helping fill this void with people who want to reach out to these orphans. Countless lesser-known ministries, children's shelters, orphanages, and churches worldwide are also stepping in to help. Still, it is an ever-present problem.

So what does this have to do with our involvement with one small boy named Chandler?

It is easy to become overwhelmed by such an enormous challenge as caring for countless orphans. I think that is why most of us do nothing when presented with a tremendously large challenge. We ask how we could ever have any impact on a problem so big. The only way I knew how to get beyond being overwhelmed by the orphan crisis was to decide that the very least I could do was to have an impact on one child, whether that was for a brief period of time or for the rest of my life. However, I soon learned that our decision would impact more than one child.

Interceding on behalf of Chandler's future

Because we had no idea how long Chandler was going to be in our lives when he was first placed with us, it would have been easy to only take care of his day-to-day needs. But I wanted to invest in him as much as I could. How do you do that with an infant? The answer is intercession—praying for another person and asking God for something that will benefit that person. In other words, you as the intercessor gain nothing. The focus is on impacting another person's life by asking God to do something for that person.

Because I did not know how long he was going to be in our home, I prayed earnestly that Chandler would know God personally at an early age. I asked God to heal any emotional damage that may have been done through his trauma. I also prayed that God would direct Chandler's destiny regardless of his upbringing.

I recognized that a family member somewhere could have been praying for Chandler in this manner, but I embraced interceding for Chandler as if it were the sole reason that he was in our home. I especially prayed for Chandler at night. Either Danielle or I would pray for him when one or the other placed him in bed at night. Then nearly every night, I would check on Chandler before I went to bed.

I would stand over his crib watching him sleep, whispering prayers of intercession. Some nights I would sit down in the rocker and listen to him breathe as I prayed for him.

This was an act of faith since there was the possibility that I would never see him again. I trusted that God would truly move in Chandler's life. I trusted that He would indeed heal his hurts and restore his future. I also believed that God would truly draw Chandler to Himself at a young age. Why did I believe this? Because I know this is the heart of my Heavenly Father. I know Him to be a Father who wants the best for His children. I know Him to be our Protector in a fallen world. I know Him to long for a relationship with each of us. And I know Him to be One who rallies to the side of the weakest and most vulnerable.

As time went on and Chandler remained with us longer, I had to be more intentional about interceding for him. The sense of urgency was wearing off. The desire did not wear off, though. I continued to check on him nearly every night before I went to bed and whispered a prayer over him.

Chandler's family

As I prayed for Chandler, I often prayed that he would influence his biological family. If he did go back to his family while he was still very young, my hope was that he would know and love God. My prayer was that because of Chandler's time with us and our intercession for him, several in his family would come to know God personally.

I think that this intercession influenced our relationship with Chandler's family. It was obvious that they felt thankful that we were taking good care of Chandler, but it seemed deeper than that from the very beginning. There was a short window of time when I thought that we would have an even deeper relationship with Chandler's family.

Initially, the CPS caseworker was working hard to move the case to reunification. She was strongly encouraging the young parents to work on the requirements that the court had mandated. She was also concerned about Chandler struggling at parent visits. He was becoming more attached to us, which for his age, this was completely normal. He was only seeing his parents for one hour each week, and sometimes they would cancel the visit. Chandler was beginning to cry for nearly the whole hour of the parent visit. The CPS caseworker decided to expand the visits to two hours. The objective was to give Chandler more time to bond with his parents.

I went with Danielle to the first two-hour parent visit. The visits were still at the drab, nondescript CPS office. We met the parents in the same waiting room while we waited for the caseworker. They enjoyed watching Chandler walk around and listening to him say a few new words. When it came time for them to take Chandler back to the visitation room, he began to cry. Danielle and I left to eat an early dinner. We learned to take advantage of opportunities to spend time together without having to set up approved babysitting.

We headed back to the CPS office before the visit was over. The parents, CPS caseworker, and Chandler met us in the lobby. We immediately realized that it had been a stressful visit. We learned that Chandler had cried nonstop for the first hour. That would stress *anyone* out. We later learned that it had concerned the CPS caseworker so much that she had tried calling us to ask if Chandler had been sick or was teething. She called our home phone, so we did not get the calls. She was looking for any reason that would explain his crying so much.

The parents were visibly troubled, especially the mom. Danielle and I began to encourage them. We let them know that we believed in them and that we were pulling for them to be successful. I doubt that they had many people, if anyone, talk to them in this manner.

Sadly, this was the last parent visit that the mother attended. Soon after that visit, she let CPS know that she did not feel fit to be Chandler's mother. We were very surprised to hear this, but I respected her maturity in making this decision. It still did not mean that we were going to be able to adopt Chandler. Chandler's father and his family were still showing interest in raising him.

We learned that the process of a family working on the state required plan for reunification with their child could be slow and complex with many suspenseful turns, and this was one of those turns. I don't know why things turn out the way they do sometimes. It looked like this young couple was going to continue to work on things. It also looked like Danielle and I might be more involved in their lives. Suddenly the path went in a totally different direction. If his parents would have followed through with the State requirements, I really do think we would have become closer to them.

At this point, we were only in contact with Chandler's father's side of the family. Even though the case was not going very smoothly for them, our interaction with them was still very positive. I was thankful because I know from other foster parents that this is not always the case.

One interaction that is seared in my mind was at the court hearing right before Christmas 2011. Danielle and I thought there was a good chance that the judge was going to order that Chandler be placed with his paternal grandmother. I think that grandmother thought the same thing, but this did not happen. I am not sure why Chandler was not placed with his grandmother, except that CPS was not convinced the home was safe for Chandler. I was standing out in the hall talking to our caseworker when Chandler's grandmother walked out toward me. Her face could not hide her disappointment, and I could not help but feel sad for her. She introduced me to her husband for the first time. Like all the other family members had before, he thanked me for taking care of Chandler. Then Chandler's grandmother said that she had some Christmas presents to pass on to me.

Of course, my main objective was the safety and well being of Chandler. However, I had gone from not wanting to even meet his family to regularly praying for them. I still think about them from time to time, and I still pray that Chandler will one day be the one to lead many of them to Christ.

Influence

I did not grasp how much our decision to foster and adopt would affect people around us. Most people tend to root for an underdog like an at-risk child, so it was natural for people to respond favorably when they learned about what we were doing.

My friend John shared a story with me one day about how an oral surgeon waived his fee for a medical procedure performed on John's adopted son. The fee was for a few thousand dollars. John expressed his surprise by the oral surgeon's actions, but like most people, the surgeon showed compassion for an orphaned child. I think that he also had respect for a family who was willing to open their lives and home to such a child.

Our decision to foster and eventually adopt has opened up numerous opportunities for us to meet and get to know many people that we probably would not have known otherwise. We would have still known others, such as some neighbors, but we wouldn't have known them as closely. We would not have met the caseworkers, attorneys, and many other foster families. Some we were only around for a few times, but others were in our home many times, and we got to know them at a deeper level. Of course, these are people who already have a heart for orphaned and vulnerable children. Over time, I became more and more sensitive to sharing our lives with them as much as possible. We had in common a compassion for at-risk children. That opened doors for us to share freely about our faith.

As for some of our neighbors, just having a child in our home has brought us closer to them. It just so happens that we have several kids on our street and around the corner from our home right now. Of course, we probably would have met them and talked from time to time, but having a child in our home gave us many more opportunities to share our lives with them.

When a person is willing to venture into a new journey, it opens up a whole new world of people to get to know. If I truly want to live a life of influence, then I need to be willing to embrace new adventures and new opportunities. By doing so, I can meet more people and hopefully live life alongside many of them. I believe that, too, is reflective of the Father's heart.

CHAPTER 16

SELFLESSNESS

I am thankful that I have been married close to 25 years, because it has rubbed off many of my rough edges, including being so stinking selfish. My sweet wife has paid quite a price at times for being my spouse. I honestly believe that marriage is not necessarily to make us happy but to make us more holy. If we allow it, marriage will sharpen, challenge, soften, and cause us to grow up. Having children surely speeds up this process, and in my case, not having children stunted some of that growth.

It was disappointing not being a father in my 20's or 30's when most have the opportunity, but I can see now that God was nurturing and cultivating in me a heart of the father through the many life experiences that I have had, both good and bad. By the time we decided to respond to the Holy Spirit's calling to foster and adopt a child or children, I was at least ready to accept the challenge. What I did not expect were the ways I would grow through the process.

Fostering is very stressful, especially emotionally. Fostering a child gave me ample opportunities to grow in ways that no other experience would have accomplished. Being 50 years old and never having had to share my space and time with a child 24/7 definitely created some selfish tendencies. I had become accustomed to doing what I wanted when I wanted with whom I wanted, without having to concern myself with anyone except Danielle. Caring for a foster child, especially one so young, drastically chipped away at my selfish core.

Do you remember me talking about Danielle's Plate Envy Disorder? Looking back, I can see how God was working on my selfish attitude. Little did I know that He was preparing me for a little boy who would also want my food and drink!

One day I was driving around with Chandler and decided to get a chocolate shake. Of course, he wanted some, too. He kept saying, "More drink that!" So there I was sharing my chocolate shake with a little toddler who was replacing the shake with his slobber. But you know what? I didn't care in the least bit.

I have watched more shows like Clifford the Big Red Dog, Thomas the Train, and Elmo than I think I did when I was a kid. I have read the same books over and over and over, which I hardly ever do on my own. I have also eaten more meals at Chik-Fil-A and McDonald's recently than I have in my whole life. My garage is filling up fast with toddler toys, pushing my possessions aside or up in the attic. I have turned one flowerbed into a sand box, and the others get trampled. I slept less during the first year that Chandler was in our home than my college years. I once was a sound sleeper, but soon after Chandler came to our home, Danielle and I decided that it would be my responsibility to get up with him at night if he cried out. In the middle of the night, I have changed dirty diapers, crawled under a crib looking for a pacifier, and wiped a runny nose.

I think you get the picture. I am learning that I have what it takes to give my life for someone else's life. I am becoming less selfish with my time, my comfort, and my possessions. At least I hope I am. Most of this was happening over several months when we did not know whether Chandler would stay with us or not.

Giving my heart to a foster child forced me to place my trust more fully in God. So much of this experience was out of my control. As a foster parent, I had very little say in what happened in Chandler's life. Leaning on Christ and abiding or resting in Him shaped me during the journey. Placing my heart in the hands of my Heavenly Father and trusting He would do what was best for all involved, I learned how to let go of what I wanted and allow Him to direct our paths.

CHAPTER 17

HOW TO LET GO

Adopting a father's heart means that you have the child's best interest in mind, even if it means that your own heart has a good chance of being hurt. This takes sacrifice. Why did I decide to take this chance? God had fostered in my heart a willingness to make sacrifices for the benefit of an orphaned child. I am willing to sacrifice my comfort, agenda, and wealth for the benefit of a child even when I know I have a good chance that I will suffer some kind of pain.

God demonstrated His heart of a father by sacrificing His only Son for our benefit. I can only imagine the amount of pain and suffering that God endured as He watched His Son be crucified on the cross. I will never have to endure that much pain, but when I agreed with Danielle to foster a child, I was opening up my heart to potential heartache. I knew that I would give a child like Chandler my heart with the possibility that he could be removed from my life.

I am reminded of the story of the two women brought before King Solomon, both claiming to be the mother of the same child. The way the true mother responded when the king suggested that the child be cut into two halves reflects the heart of a parent who is willing to let go of her child for what is best for the child. She was willing to let her child go with the other woman in order for him to live. However, her response revealed to King Solomon who the real mother of this child was. It was the one with a true mother's heart that wanted what was best for her child even though it meant pain and suffering for herself.

Having a heart that wants the best for our children means that we must learn to let them go, even if it does cause us great pain.

Opening Our Hearts to Foster

When Danielle and I decided to foster, we knew that we would likely face a day when we would have to let go of a child. Ideally, every foster child returns to their family or is adopted by another family. When we agreed to the placement of Chandler in our home, we completely understood that it was a foster placement. From the very beginning of our relationship, I began preparing myself for the day when I would have to let go of Chandler. I knew that was not going to be easy. Whenever we had days or even weeks without having parent visits or interaction with CPS, it was easy to forget that I was only Chandler's foster dad. I thought and felt as if I were his biological father and that he would be with us forever. I tried to not concern myself with what the future would look like.

As Chandler's case progressed, I continued to adapt how I prepared myself for letting him go. During the first few months, I really thought that he would leave our family any day. What was my great plan to let Chandler go? Remain as uninvolved with his case as possible. That is why I did not attend the first court hearing. Why get involved with the case or his family if Chandler was only going to be with us for a few weeks? This plan of action, I hoped, would protect my heart.

He Could Leave Any Day

When Chandler was first placed with us, I felt strongly that Chandler should reunite with his family. If he were my son or grandson, I would want him to stay in our family, without a doubt. Some of my family members asked me about this. In one sense, only God knew what was best for Chandler. However, when I put myself in his family's shoes, I could not fathom giving him up for adoption to strangers, not if we had the means to take care of him. In Chandler's case, I really did think that his extended family had the means to keep him and raise him. I responded to those questions by asking what *they* would do or want to see happen if one of their unmarried children or grandchildren had a baby. Would they suggest that the baby be put up for adoption or would they want someone in our family to raise that child?

In my opinion, it is quite different if a foster child comes from a family that is completely broken down. One in which there is continual abuse and neglect. One in which no one is willing or able to care for the child. One in which there is a good chance that the child could be abandoned. For families like this, most would suggest that the parental rights be terminated and a loving and capable family adopt the child. However, I struggled with what seemed to be happening in Chandler's case. I am resistant to any government agency overstepping its rights to infringe on the rights of people. After Chandler was placed with us, ironically, I found myself on the other side of the fence. Out of my desire to care for vulnerable children, I had become involved in a case in which a government agency had removed a child from a family and placed him into the custody of the state. The state government who would ultimately determine the future of Chandler's life.

I had no doubt that Chandler had sustained traumatic injuries from someone in his family. I completely agree that CPS needed to investigate. What I was not sure about was why Chandler was not placed with another family member. It seemed to me to be an overreaction by CPS. I realize that I did not have all the facts and that I am a novice when it comes to matters such as this one. However, it seemed to me that it was a bit too easy for a family's child to be taken away from everyone in the family. I struggled with this for a while. Because of my convictions about cases like this, I thought that someone in Chandler's family would step forward to take custody of him. Surely the courts would agree. Even though this was no longer a theoretical scenario for me, I could not insist that Chandler stay with us, but because I was being a father to this young child, it was only going to make it more difficult for me to let him go. I had to trust that God was in control of the situation, even over government entities. Aside from my personal internal struggle with Chandler's case, here we were with this incredibly precious little boy in our home. I could tell that my heart was quickly attaching to him. I was trying hard to find a delicate balance of loving this child as my own and being ready for him to go back to his family at any time.

Along with the birth parent visits, the court hearings became reminders of the impending temporary nature of our relationship with Chandler as parents. We knew that Chandler would not go back to his parents before December 2011, but I felt that any day CPS was going to call us to let us know that a grandparent, an uncle, or some other family member was going to take custody of Chandler. I continued to make an attempt to protect my heart for that potential day.

During those first few months, people would often ask us if we thought that we would be able to adopt Chandler. Especially in the beginning, this was a difficult question for me. I guess people did not quite understand that at the time we were simply fostering Chandler, or maybe they didn't know what that meant. I would try to reply as kindly as I could that Chandler was a foster child, and that adoption was not a part of the plan. Our friends knew that we were interested in adopting a child, so I guess it was natural for them to wonder if we would be able to adopt Chandler. However, I could not help but be frustrated by the questions. Chandler's parents and extended family seemed to love and want him. It was hard for me to entertain the possibility of adopting him. The questions from well-meaning friends only reminded me that he was not my son. My desire was to raise him as if he were my son each and every day he was with us. If and when the day came to let him go, I would hopefully rest in God's grace at that time. If I thought too much about the possibility of Chandler leaving our family, I became despondent, frustrated, and even depressed, and that was not healthy for any of us. After a while, I began to tell others that it was a one in a million chance that we would ever be able to adopt Chandler.

Time Marched On

Weeks turned into months as the December 2011 court date approached. Chandler had his weekly parent visits that were usually traumatic for him. The parent visits at the CPS office were the hardest.

The traumatic pattern usually started with Chandler crying when we handed him off to his parents. Many times he would cry for most of or the entire parent visit. When I think about that now, it seems odd that he would cry when he would see his own family. On the drive home, he would usually fall asleep. For a while the visits were around lunchtime, so we would take something for him to eat after his visit before we drove home. Then, we could simply transfer him to his crib when we got home if he was still asleep. For the next couple of days after a visit, Chandler would be more fussy than usual, become upset if either of us left, and would wake up in the night more frequently. After a couple days, he would settle down a bit only for it to start all over again a few days later at the next parent visit.

Even though the visits were scheduled weekly, it was not uncommon for the parents to not show up or to cancel the visit. As we got closer to the court date in December 2011, Chandler's parents missed three or four visits in a row. In some ways, I was glad when this happened because Chandler would not go through his routine of traumatic behavior. However, I was also sad that his parents would so easily miss an opportunity to see their son. As the weeks turned into months, I had to continue to adapt. In the first several weeks that we had Chandler, it was a little easier to tell myself that he was not my son, that his family loved and wanted him, that I was just providing some stability in his young life that would hopefully benefit him later. But the longer Chandler was with us, the easier it was to think of him as my own son. Around this time, Chandler's mother told Danielle that she wanted us to continue seeing Chandler after he moved back home with her. I know that Chandler's mother was complimenting us, but this was very hard for Danielle. She cried all the way home.

The holiday season was fast approaching, and it was beginning to look like Chandler would be with us at least through Thanksgiving. My family had been going to the coast for Thanksgiving for the past several years. As they began making plans, they asked if Chandler would be coming with us. We really did not know. Of course, if he were still a part of our family, we would get permission from his CPS caseworker for him to go with us. That was how life was for us. Anytime we made any plans to take a trip out of town, we had to inform our CPS caseworker. She needed to know where we were going, how long we would be there, who we would be with, and so on. We could arrange for Chandler to stay with another foster care family if we so chose, but because we always treated him like he was our own son, we never considered leaving him with other foster families. Still, whenever we were making plans, we always had to keep in mind that Chandler might be gone by the time the trip arrived. As for the Thanksgiving week at the beach, we did not know what state of mind we would be in. We could have been loading our car down with stuff for a 13-month-old or it could have been just the two of us. If it had been just Danielle and I, we most likely would have been in a state of shock about Chandler leaving our family.

A couple weeks before Thanksgiving, we received an email that served as a painful reminder that Chandler could be leaving our family soon. The email requested that we complete a questionnaire as Chandler's caregivers. The purpose of the questionnaire was to identify issues and needs that Chandler had. This would assist the potential new caregivers for Chandler. It included questions about Chandler's eating habits, bedtime routine, kinds of activities, etc. The last question was, "What role did we want to play in the pre-placement process?" I tried not to let the questionnaire bother me. *I* wanted to be Chandler's caregiver. *I* wanted to be his father!

Another Family Meeting

A few weeks before the December court hearing, there was another family meeting. Again, they requested that we bring Chandler with us. Because of how the first meeting went, I was not looking forward to this one. The setting was much the same, except that one family member and the father's lawyer were not present. Chandler was just beginning to take a few steps and could walk holding onto furniture. While we waited in the lobby for the meeting to begin, his family was enjoying watching him walk awkwardly around the room.

When the CPS caseworkers were ready for us, we all filed into the conference room and sat in the exact same seats that we did for the first meeting nearly five months earlier. Being a typical 13-month-old, Chandler was having a hard time sitting still, so Danielle and I took turns walking around the room with him. Just like the first meeting, we did not say anything. The emotions were even more intense this time around. Chandler's parents were not dating anymore, so that made the situation more complex. Neither parent was completing their required steps for reunification. They had even missed a few recent parent visits. This is when we found out that Chandler's mother did not feel that she could adequately care for Chandler. She did not want her rights terminated, but she did not want to be the primary caregiver either. She actually stated that she felt that he was in a good place with us. I was not sure what this would all mean, but I could sense a major shift beginning to take place. The CPS caseworkers commended her for being mature in her decision. I agree that Chandler's mother was making a mature decision about her inability to care for her son.

Chandler's father and paternal grandmother still wanted custody of Chandler. From that day forward, we only dealt with Chandler's father and his family. My heart hurt for Chandler's mother. Even though I was deeply attached to Chandler by this time, I was also hoping that his parents could get their acts together for Chandler's sake. If the court was going to reunite Chandler with his parents or place him with a family member, I wanted them to be successful. Now that Chandler's mother had decided not to pursue being his primary caregiver, I was not sure what to think. That day was the last day she saw her son before her parental rights were terminated several months later.

Chandler Joins Us for the Holidays

The week after that second family meeting, we packed up our car until there was no more space in it and headed to the beach for a week. Yes, Chandler was going with us! We had a great time, as he enjoyed playing in the sand and playing with his cousins, aunts and uncles, and grandparents. Getting to experience the beach as a 13-month-old baby boy seemed to be a wonderful treat. It was a special treat for a grateful father as well. We spent five days at the beach with my family. Then we spent three more days with Danielle's mom who lived nearby before we headed back home. It took us about another week back at home to retrain our young foster son to not expect several people doting over him nonstop!

It was fun spending that time with family away from the constant reminders of Chandler being only our foster son, but the court hearing scheduled for December 2011 was just a few days after we returned home. If I was going to have to let him go, I wanted to do everything in my power to have a positive influence on his future. We really thought that the judge would grant custody of Chandler to his grandmother at this time since it was just a couple of weeks before Christmas. Because the parents had not been accomplishing their mandated requirements, it was clear that Chandler was not going to reunite with either of them for at least another six months.

I had been trying to prepare myself for Chandler being placed with a family member by Christmastime, so when that didn't happen, I was really surprised. Chandler had just celebrated his first birthday with us. He had gone to the beach with us for Thanksgiving, and now he would be celebrating Christmas with us as well. When we saw our families at Thanksgiving, they asked us if we thought Chandler would still be with us at Christmas, a question for which we had no answer. When they heard that he would be present after all, they were excited to get to see him again. By now our extended family was starting to get used to him being around. Chandler got presents from his biological family, Danielle's family, my family, CPS, and Arrow. We rationed the toys over several weeks so that he would not overdose on new toys!

We spent one day with my family and one with Danielle's family over Christmas. He had great time! Of course, our families enjoyed having him around as well, but in some ways it was bittersweet for me, because it felt like I was only playing house. Surely, I thought, Chandler was not going to be with us for any more Christmases after this one.

Struggling to Adapt

As the New Year began with Chandler still in our home, I knew that my heart was becoming strongly intertwined with his. The first week of January 2012 Chandler had a parent visit. His paternal grandmother had begun making the visits along with Chandler's father. It seemed even more likely that Chandler would end up being placed with her. I wrote the following in my journal: "I think (the parent visit) was hard for me because it was staring the probable outcome in the face. I become more attached to Chandler every day. I think and act like I am his father. Lord, continue to give me all that I need. Continue to protect my heart so that I can love with abandon." Two days later I wrote, "I have been struggling the past two days since the parent visit. Chandler is really struggling. He is fussier during the day. He cries more at night, and he tests his boundaries more. This makes me angry with his family. Still, I know that he is more than likely going back to his family. Lord, keep my heart tender in spite of the pain. Help me not to escape or withdraw." I prayed prayers like this all the time, hoping that if Chandler left our family, my heart would be ready.

Chandler was beginning to look and act more and more like a little boy instead of a baby. He was walking everywhere instead of crawling. His hair was getting longer and fuller. He was also learning how to let his thoughts and wishes be known. I was enjoying all of this. I never expected to to see him progress from one stage to another. His personality was beginning to blossom. We were finding out that he was a social little guy. He loved to hug other little people. One day at an indoor playground, he saw a little girl not much older than he was. I guess he thought she was pretty because he started walking toward her with his arms open wide. He had not been walking for long, so it was more like a waddle. As he waddled toward the little girl with his arms open, she began backing up with a concerned look on her face. She seemed unsure about what Chandler's intentions were. About the time he reached her, she stumbled and fell softly backwards with Chandler falling right on top of her. No one was hurt, but Chandler's attempt to hug her turned into a slow-motion tackle. I loved every second of it, even though the little girl's parents probably thought we were both nuts. I was enjoying the fact that God was being gracious giving me moments like this to experience as Chandler's father.

As the first several weeks of the new year turned into a couple of months, it still looked as if Chandler would be going back to someone in his family, even though he had been with us for nearly nine months. The longer Chandler stayed with us, the harder it was going to be to let him go. His grandmother's husband began attending some of the parent visits now. It was good to see their desire to spend time with Chandler, but it was also another reminder that not only was I not Chandler's father. I was not even a blood relative.

In light of what I was seeing from Chandler's father and grandmother at the parent visits, I did not understand why CPS had not already moved Chandler to the grandmother's home. Apparently CPS had some concerns and was not in any hurry to move him. I think they saw how well Chandler seemed to be doing in our home. I appreciate the fact that CPS (at least those we were dealing with) wanted to avoid as much disruption for a child as possible. The last thing anyone wanted to do was to move Chandler to another home if there was any chance that he would not remain there.

Around this time, Danielle shared with me that she really wanted to be a mother—Chandler's mother. One thing that I appreciate about Danielle is her ability and willingness to share what she is feeling. However, it drove home the reality of what was happening to our hearts. We both had adopted this little boy into our hearts, and if he left, it was going to hurt like crazy!

A Major Shift

By the time Chandler had been with us for ten months, he had lived with us longer than he had with anyone in his family. It is important for a baby to bond with his mother and father. Children that do not bond when they are a baby with a parent figure usually suffer with attachment disorders well into their adulthood. From day one, we had treated Chandler as if he were our biological son. As a result Chandler knew us as his daddy and mommy. He was beginning to talk, and he was calling us daddy and mommy. I don't know how we could have prevented that from happening, short of acting like we were only his babysitters.

About this time, CPS began making some changes to the plan for family reunification. The original plan was for Chandler to be reunified with one or both of his parents, but neither parent was pursuing this plan of action. Every time I think about that, my heart hurts. We most definitely were ready and willing to adopt Chandler, but it was still painful for me to see his family fail at meeting the CPS requirements. Because the parents were not meeting or pursuing any of the state mandated requirements, CPS recommended to the judge that the plan be changed. The recommendation was for Plan A to be relative adoption and Plan B to be non-relative adoption. For the first time since Chandler had been with us, the possibility of us adopting him developed.

Initially, I thought that this shift in the case would make it harder for me to stay in the moment without getting my hopes up. I hoped that I would be able to stay engaged with Chandler instead of pulling away in order to protect my heart. God proved to be faithful. He gave me the ability to love Chandler as my own son. Now when people would ask me if I thought that we would be able to adopt Chandler, my response was that it was now a two in a million chance. The odds had doubled! It was still a long shot, but I was willing to at least entertain the possibility that I would not have to let Chandler go anytime soon.

However, as I allowed this possibility to gain a foothold in my heart, I continued to have reminders of the probable outcome. For example, one day I went with Danielle to a supervised parent visit at a local mall. I was watching from the car as Danielle picked Chandler up after the visit. The CPS worker was standing close by supervising the hand off. Chandler's young father came out the door of the mall pushing Chandler's stroller. Following closely behind Chandler's father came Chandler's grandmother, step-grandfather, and a few other family members. I watched as Chandler's father picked him up out of the stroller and walked a few feet away to tell him goodbye. Chandler had seen Danielle walk up and was reaching out for her. Danielle introduced herself to the family members that she had not met yet and stood by talking with them for a minute. They each took turns kissing Chandler goodbye. Then they handed him over to Danielle, who quickly walked to our car. I felt my heart pound hard in my chest as I watched this scene. It seemed obvious that Chandler's family loved him. I knew that they wanted to do what was right. I knew he was their kin. If the court decided that it was best for Chandler to live with someone in his family, or to be adopted by another family for that matter, then I would have to let him go.

A friend of ours who has fostered several children and has adopted a few told us that letting go of a foster child is very similar to losing a biological child. My hands froze after writing that sentence. I think of the few people I know who have lost a child and how hard that was on them and their marriage. I did not want to be naive nor anxious about what could be ahead.

Each night before I would go to bed, I quietly walked into Chandler's room to check on him and watch him sleep for a few minutes. I think I could have stood there for an hour on some nights. He still looked like a little baby, but he also looked more like a little boy. It caused me to wonder what his life would be like as he grew up. If he left our family, I wondered if he would remember us. If he did remember us, what would he remember? Would he remember the sound of my voice, the way I looked at him, the things I said to him, or my praying over him? What would he be like when he started school? What would his personality be like? What kinds of interests would he have? Would we stay in touch with him? Should we stay in touch with him? As I wrote these things, I felt the sadness in my heart and the tears building in my eyes. God had been teaching me to lean into the emotions I felt instead of avoiding or running away from them, but this was a tough emotion to not push away and ignore.

Sometimes I thought about what it would be like to take down his crib, give away his outgrown toys and clothes, and unlock the kitchen cabinets. If he left, I hoped that I would be able to grieve his leaving in a healthy manner. Honestly, I was not sure if I would be able to foster again. I also was aware that as long as I walked with God through the pain, He would mend my broken heart and prepare me for whatever was next, even if it meant giving my heart to another foster child. For whatever was next, I wanted to be able to continue opening my heart to whatever God wanted to do.

It all boiled down to what was best for Chandler, regardless of my attachment to him. I knew that after he had lived with us for several months, I would have given my life for him. Honestly, I was that willing a few weeks after he came into my life.

What an incredible lesson God had taught me through this experience. He taught me how to love a child with sacrificial love. Love that dared to put my heart out there to be painfully hurt. I do not think that kind of love exists in my own heart of flesh. My heart had to adopt the heart of my Father in order to love like that.

ADOPTION

CHAPTER 18

PARENTAL RIGHTS
TERMINATED

After the plan was altered to reflect a new Plan A, relative or kinship adoption, and a new Plan B, non-relative adoption, CPS also canceled all parent visits. I was not sure whether CPS would have allowed any of Chandler's extended family to have a visit after this decision, but regardless, that never happened.

The last time Chandler saw anyone from his family was when he was nearly 16 months old—about three months before the next court hearing. He had lived with us for half of his life by that time. I was in shock about what was happening.

When the day of the hearing arrived, I made my now-familiar trek to the courthouse. Sadly, no one from Chandler's family showed up. Our CPS caseworker had informed us that CPS was going to recommend to the judge that the parental rights be terminated. Some of the extended family had shown some interest in obtaining custody of Chandler, but after a home study, CPS was not recommending this action either. I arrived at the courthouse a few minutes before the docket of cases was scheduled to begin. I was becoming more accustomed to the proceedings and participants involved in the hearings. I took a seat next to our Arrow caseworker—a few rows back from the front—and waited for things to begin. This day things got started a little later than usual, so I prepared myself for a long morning. I greeted Chandler's lawyer, his CPS caseworker, and the mother's attorney with a nod. The usual scurrying around and whispers filled the courtroom.

Finally, the judge began hearing the cases. Chandler's case came up rather quickly, much to my surprise. I looked around the courtroom again to see if Chandler's family had come in without my noticing. None of them were there. I felt a twinge of sadness and a little confusion. The judge called for Chandler's case. All the attorneys and CPS caseworkers involved with his case made their way to the front of the courtroom. Our Arrow caseworker and I moved up to the first row so we could hear what was being said. The case began just like all the others. The county attorney asked the CPS caseworker some standard questions about Chandler's current placement and well-being. Then there were the usual questions about the parents' adherence to the court's mandated plan for them. The caseworker reported that in general the parents had not continued working the plan and that they had not returned any of her attempts to contact them. Both of the parents' attorneys asked some clarifying questions in an attempt to represent their client in some kind of positive light.

Then Chandler's attorney spoke. She made it clear that in her opinion the parents had been given plenty of opportunities to show their desire to be reunified to their child and had failed. She went on to point out that they knew about the current court hearing but apparently decided not to attend. She concurred with the CPS caseworker and the parents' attorneys that the parents understood that CPS was recommending that their parental rights be terminated.

Finally she asked the judge to not delay the decision until another hearing and to terminate their rights immediately. The judge paused for a few seconds, then stated that he was ready to terminate the parents' rights, but first he wanted to make sure that they were not on the premises. He asked the bailiff to walk out into the hallway and call for each parent. The courtroom was perfectly quiet as everyone heard the bailiff walk out of the courtroom into the hallway and first call out Chandler's mother's name. His voice echoed down the large, long hallway. One, two, three times he called out her name. Then he did the same for Chandler's father. I felt a lump form in my throat as the weight of what was happening hit me. How could they not show up, I wondered. Would they not fight for this child?

The bailiff reentered the courtroom to inform the judge that no one replied. Then, the judge made it official. The parents' rights were terminated. He made some concluding comments to the attorneys that I could not fully hear or understand. The attorneys then filed out as our Arrow caseworker turned to me, saying how exciting that was for us. In that moment, I could not feel her same excitement. It was all too bittersweet for me. Of course, I was excited that we were closer to being able to adopt Chandler, but I was also so sad for his parents and extended family. I felt as if they were in effect giving up on him. They were abandoning him.

I got up and walked out into the hallway, asking our Arrow caseworker if I understood correctly what had just happened. Then Chandler's attorney walked out. The first thing she said to me was, "Ok, let's get this moving!" Since I was in a bit of a state of shock, I replied, "Excuse me?" She repeated herself, and then she explained that the parents' rights were indeed terminated. I asked her about the parents' right to appeal, and I verbally wondered what rights the extended family had. She informed me that the parents had 30 days to appeal and that the extended family also had a window of time to ask for custody. In her estimation, neither would happen.

I left the courtroom still numb by what had just taken place. I walked to my truck, and then I called Danielle to let her know what had happened. Her response was very similar to mine—bittersweet. On the one hand we were excited that it now looked like we would be able to adopt Chandler. On the other hand, we felt sad that his family had not tried harder to keep him.

Now when people asked us if we would be able to adopt Chandler, I responded with guarded optimism. I was finally allowing my heart to entertain the idea that we could end up adopting Chandler, though there was still a window of time in which someone could enter the picture and take custody of him. I needed to remain open to the idea that we might still have to let him go. If that happened, how would I be able to let him go without completely shutting down? I was not sure. I would have to go through a grieving process. Then I hoped that I would get up, brush myself off, and move on. I hoped to have God's grace and favor to be able to do so.

CHAPTER 19

FAVOR

As I look back over this journey that we have traveled over the past three years, I notice a pattern rising to the surface, although it was not always as clear while I was in the middle of the journey. In a word, the pattern is best described as favor—God's favor to be specific.

I became a Christ follower at a young age, but it has taken my whole life to understand my identity in Christ. I now understand that I belong to Christ. For many years I struggled with the notion that I could receive unmerited favor. I understood it intellectually, but my thoughts and actions betrayed me. Either I did not truly believe it or was unwilling to receive it. I do not think that I am unique in this struggle.

So, what am I talking about? I believe that all of creation receives a level of God's favor or grace. If it were not so, we would all quickly face destruction by the hand of nature, by other people, or by our own doing. God compassionately extends His favor toward His creation. He has His reasons. One very big reason is that He wants each of us to know Him. If and when we do surrender our lives to Him, I believe that this favor increases in its intensity. His favor shifts from being general in nature to becoming more intimate and focused on us because we become His adopted sons and daughters. We also become joint heirs with Christ. God's favor toward us is now tied to our new place in His family.

It has taken me years to accept this truth. My tendency has been to allow my decisions and actions to affect how I viewed my place in His family. When I view my relationship with God through the lens of my failures, I tell myself that I do not deserve His favor. I have even seen myself self-destruct, almost begging to be punished because I knew that I deserved it. In fact, I would anticipate bad things happening to me as a means of punishment. Thankfully, He has gently shown me the lens through which He views our relationship. I understand today that He sees me as His adopted son who is a joint heir to His Kingdom with Christ Jesus.

I do not think that this gives me license to sin and rebel against His ways. The apostle Paul was clear about this when he wrote, "What shall we say then? Are we to continue in sin so that grace may increase? May it never be!" (Romans 6:1-2a) I do think that there are consequences to poor, sinful choices. In fact, someone has to be punished. But this is the perfect definition of favor and grace. When I deserved to be punished for my sin and rebellion, God Himself took on that punishment through Jesus Christ. Now when God looks at me, He does not see my sin; He sees the selfless act of His very own Son. Therefore, His desire is to continue to pour out favor on my life as His adopted son. What does all of this have to do with our experience of fostering? Through the journey of fostering and eventually adopting Chandler, I have seen this favor play out in many ways in our life.

Holding Loosely

For about the past ten years, Danielle and I have tried to hold loosely the things of this world. We are blessed and grateful for everything that God has given us. That is exactly how we view our possessions and our very life. They are His, not ours. I do not even attribute the decision to live this way as my brilliant idea. I believe God desires us to live this way. As we have held our possessions loosely, I have cared less and less about what the world calls success. I see our possessions as tools to be used for His purposes, not as status symbols. I see our relationships as gifts from God to be treated with care, but I do not allow them to control my life and my decisions. Living this way has brought me freedom. How does this apply to fostering, adoption, and God's favor?

When I make my relationship with Him my priority, then the things of this world become less important. I understand Whose they really are. It further opens my heart to the idea of sharing not only my possessions but also my life with someone who needs them. I believe that as I live my life in this way, God's favor flows more freely. I do not think that His grace is a reward for living right. Instead, I see it more like a conduit that is not clogged with earthly desires. Not only does God's favor have a positive effect on our lives, but it also begins to have a positive effect on those with whom we come in contact. This is not a formula; it is a way of life.

Chandler's Placement

How have I seen God's favor during this journey of fostering and adopting? Let's think about the slim chances that a child would be placed in our home in the first place. If you will remember, Danielle and I were not interested in foster care. We only wanted to adopt. If we had remained steadfast in that desire, then Arrow would never have called us. Chandler was a foster placement.

Also, even after we had decided to foster, we turned down several placement opportunities. Even though I felt bad each time we turned down a placement, I think this was God's providence and favor. If we would have had another child or two to three children in our home, we would never have accepted the placement of Chandler. We probably would not even have been called.

Then, you will remember that when I received the call for Chandler, I was a little hesitant to accept him because he was so young, and I could not reach Danielle, but I had no other reason for not accepting his placement. I made the decision to accept his placement, having no idea what it would be like to have such a young child in our home. I also did not know how long he would be with us. I came very close to turning down the placement of Chandler because he was only eight-months-old.

What I did not consider in that brief moment of decision-making was how God had placed in our lives several families with preschool-age children. These families ended up being a Godsend as they immediately provided items needed to care for a baby. They also provided emotional support, from mothers who were at the very same stage of life. I do not consider that to be a coincidence. I call that God's favor.

Chandler's Family

I was hoping that we would not have to interact with Chandler's family. In fact, I was hoping that we would not even meet them. My fear was that Chandler's family would direct their anger about the situation towards us. I was also concerned that they might think that we wanted to take their baby away from them. My fears turned out to be unfounded because every interaction that we had with every family member was always positive. Later, when we had access to the case file, I learned that Chandler's mother liked Danielle the first time she met her. Her comment was that she did not feel looked down upon by Danielle. She also did not feel that Danielle was trying to "take away her baby." I cannot imagine what it is like to see your child for only one hour a week and see them leave with another family. Even when it looked less likely that anyone in Chandler's family was going to get custody of him, the family still treated us with respect. They continued to express their appreciation about the care we were giving him. It could easily have been a lot different. Again, I see God's favor in how Chandler's family received us. I think the favor we had with the family heavily influenced the parents allowing their parental rights to be terminated.

CPS and Chandler's *Ad Litem* Lawyer

When Danielle and I were going through our training, we heard stories about how difficult it could be working with CPS. I do not have a lot of experience, but our interaction with CPS was nothing but great. During the first few months, our conversations with our caseworker were mostly professional in nature. I could tell that the caseworker had a very heavy caseload. In fact, the first few times that we talked about

Chandler, she kept getting him confused with another case involving a child of a similar age. It was also clear that her main objective was to help the parents or another family member regain custody of Chandler as soon as possible.

I think that Chandler's caseworker initially viewed us simply as Chandler's temporary custodians. However, as time went on and we saw his caseworker nearly every week at parent visits or home visits, we got to know her better. A huge turning point was when she got an email from Chandler's doctor in response to some information that she needed. The doctor gave us high praise for the job we were doing with Chandler. I think that as the caseworker saw how we took care of Chandler, she began to understand that we really did care for him and wanted whatever was best for him, even if that meant he would return to his family. Over time, we began to see a big difference in how she related to us. I could clearly see God's favor once again. On one home visit, Danielle met our caseworker at the door. Immediately, Danielle could tell that something was upsetting her. Danielle asked if she was OK. With tears in her eyes, the caseworker replied that she had just come from a difficult home visit. We do not know what happened and never will. All the cases are confidential, but instinctively Danielle gave her a hug and communicated how sorry she was. Not only did we care for Chandler and his family, but also the CPS caseworkers as well.

We met Chandler's *ad litem* attorney lawyer early on in his placement. She arranged for a home visit just a couple weeks after he was placed with us. I remember wondering what she was thinking. She did not say a lot, but I could tell that she was analyzing us, our home, and how we related to Chandler. I learned later that her first impression of us was positive. Again, we were experiencing God's favor.

As Chandler's case proceeded, I saw how his attorney had profound influence on the outcome. Over the course of the case, I only interacted occasionally with the attorney. Most of the interactions occurred at status hearings at the county courthouse. As it began to look like Chandler could possibly become available for adoption, I wondered more about how Danielle and I were perceived as potential forever parents for Chandler. We had never had children. I was nearly 50 years older than Chandler. Danielle and I had gone through our own marriage challenges, and we had our own set of challenges and dysfunction. What did they see when they looked at us? Even though those thoughts went through my mind, I was at peace with whatever God wanted to do. If Chandler was supposed to be in our family forever, then I believed that God would grant us favor in the eyes of those who were making these decisions. It turned out that Chandler's *ad litem* attorney was wholeheartedly in favor of us adopting him.

Bonding

As I mentioned before, it is natural for a child to bond with his main caregivers when he is a few months old, so it was not surprising that Chandler was bonding with us. However, I was surprised at how quickly he bonded with us. Chandler had seemed to attach to Danielle the day he was placed with us. He even began to cry when she left the room. I do not pretend to understand why. I just know what I observed. Those first few weeks could have been a lot different as Chandler adjusted to being in a home of complete strangers. Granted, he did not sleep well at first, but during the day he was not upset and was even calm when he was with us. I think God gave him a sense of peace and comfort with us.

You may also remember how Chandler cried at his parent visits. I will never forget the blank expression on his face as he watched his parents walk away after that first parent visit. I always thought that was strange. In retrospect, I see it as another way that God was granting us favor. God knew that Chandler was going to end up in our family forever. He knew that it was important for Chandler to bond with us as his parents at this young age. I have learned that whether or not a child bonds with parents or caregivers at that critical stage of life will affect him for the rest of his life. If we had acted toward Chandler as if we were only his temporary day care providers, and he continued to struggle with bonding with his parents during their parent visits, he would have not bonded with anyone during those crucial months. I am thankful that God impressed on our hearts to risk great pain in order to bond with Chandler, knowing that it would hurt like crazy if he had returned to his family. But God honored our sacrificial love.

Time

After I resigned from the staff position at our church at the beginning of 2011, I spent some time praying about what I wanted to do next. I considered returning to the corporate world, joining another church staff, or going into business for myself. I even considered buying one or two rental properties to manage. Eventually, I decided to begin my career as an author. I have a few books that I want to write. Before Chandler was placed with us, I began to outline some ideas. I knew nothing about how to become an author, so I began researching how to write, publish, and market a book. What first was a bit unsettling turned out to be a pure blessing.

Most days I work from home, so Chandler gets to see me all the time. What a blessing for a little guy who began his life in an unstable situation to now have two parents around a lot. Some days I am away from the house most of the day either out of necessity or by choice, but on most days I am just a few feet away from Chandler and Danielle. I take advantage of every opportunity when Danielle needs or wants to do something away from home during the day. Chandler and I hang out together playing in his room or at a park. I think one of his first words that he said was "Whataburger." That was because we ate lunch there together many times.

If I had been working full-time somewhere, I would not have been able to spend all that time with Chandler when he was first placed with us. I know that the privilege of working for myself at home is because of God's favor. He has blessed us financially and taught us how to be good stewards of what He has provided.

Adoption

When we were told after our home study that CPS probably would likely never select us to straight adopt a foster child, I thought it could take a few years, if ever, for us to adopt. I resigned myself to fostering some children without ever adopting. I guess I could have simply moved onto something else, reverting to the notion that I was not one of those "special" people who were cut out for fostering and adopting. I came very close to making that decision, especially after turning down several foster placements. However, my heart was being changed through the process. Instead of being locked into adoption, I had become willing to lay my heart on the line for a foster child or children who needed me, regardless of the outcome. My convictions had eventually become my heart. I was beginning to see the fruit of adopting the heart of a father.

Then, this precious eight-month-old boy was placed in our home. We had our very first foster placement. As I look back over the time from when Chandler was placed with us to the day we adopted him, almost 15 months to the day, I can see how God's hand was orchestrating the whole thing.

Describing the last 90 days in 2012, the time between when the parental rights were terminated and the day we adopted Chandler, demonstrates His grace in detail. These three months were a blur. Each day seemed to drag by painfully slowly. Rationally I understood that anything could still happen. The parents had 30 days to appeal. Then even though it was never exactly clear why, we were told that the state had to wait an additional 60 days, 90 days altogether before Chandler could be released for adoption. My understanding was that anyone in the extended family or even a close family friend could petition the court during this time to be considered as temporary and eventually permanent guardians for Chandler.

After Chandler's parent's rights had been terminated, the case moved from foster care to adoption services. The case was assigned a new caseworker who worked with adoptions. We stayed in close contact with our CPS caseworkers. We also communicated regularly with our new adoption attorney and Chandler's *ad litem* attorney. Having all of these people focused on making our adoption of Chandler a reality seemed strange yet encouraging.

Some days I wondered whether we needed to be doing something more to prepare, but our adoption lawyer kept telling us that all we needed to do was wait for the 90-day window to close. Finally, the 90 days were over. No one had heard a thing from anyone in Chandler's family. On the one hand, I find that very sad. On the other hand, it completely opened the door for us to proceed with adopting Chandler, and we hoped that the adoption would happen quickly.

We originally thought the adoption would happen in September 2012, but through correspondence with our adoption lawyer, we learned that it probably would not happen until October. We were a little disappointed, but I told myself, "What was a few weeks of waiting compared to a lifetime with Chandler?" Just about the time we had accepted that the adoption would not happen until sometime in October, we got a call from our adoption lawyer. It had only been a week after the 90 days were over. She asked us if we were open to having the adoption hearing the following Friday, just a few days later in September after all. Yes, of course, we were!

Everything was falling into place for us to have the adoption hearing in September as we had originally hoped. In order for this to happen, our CPS adoption caseworker had to make a third and final visit to our home, adoption papers had to be signed, and the case needed to be filed with the court. Our Arrow caseworker had already set up a visit at our home and invited the CPS caseworker. The court hearing was scheduled for the next day. At the meeting in our home, I learned that usually the final home visit and paper signing took place a few weeks before the adoption hearing. Here we were, doing this all on the day before the adoption hearing. It was like someone had expedited the entire process. Once again, I thanked God for His favor. I would have been OK with waiting for another three to six weeks if we needed to, but I was extremely thankful to have the adoption finalized.

Adoption Hearing

Even though the adoption hearing came about very quickly, several of our family and friends were able to attend the hearing. This show of support meant a lot to Danielle and me. We arrived at the courthouse about 30 minutes before the court docket was scheduled to begin. We did not want to be late! Our adoption attorney met us in the hallway and informed us how the proceeding would take place. Our case was at the top of the docket, so we should not have to wait very long. Our friends and family began showing up as soon as we arrived. Before long, we were talking and laughing and chasing Chandler around in the wide, long hallway outside the courtroom. Chandler did not understand why we were there, but he knew we were going to see a judge. He was eager to get into that courtroom so he could say "Hi" to the judge.

Finally, it was our turn, so we all filed into the courtroom. It was the same courtroom that I had been in for each of Chandler's status hearings, the same one that I found intriguing because of the different characters involved in family court, the same one where just a few months earlier I had sat listening to the bailiff bellow out the names of Chandler's parents before the judge ordered that their rights be terminated. On this day, however, I hardly noticed the other people sitting in the courtroom waiting for their case to be called. I did not feel the sadness in the room. I only felt the joy for what was about to take place in our lives. One by one, all of us, including our family and friends, made our way into the room and straight up to the front to stand before the judge.

As soon as we were all in our places, the judge asked everyone, including our family and friends, to raise our right hands to take an oath. As we were taking the oath, Chandler decided he had had enough. He was ready to get down and explore his new environment like any two-year-old boy would want to do. As our adoption attorney asked everyone questions and then me about our ability and willingness to adopt Chandler as our son, Chandler was running around exploring the courtroom. We suddenly heard a loud thud that came from the direction where Chandler was playing. He had been sitting in a chair in the jury box and had decided that he was ready to come back to where we were standing. He scooted out of the chair but misjudged the fact that he was on a small step. He made a dramatic face plant flat on the floor. That was the thud, followed by a loud cry. That brought the proceedings to a complete halt as everyone reached out toward Chandler. A friend of ours, who was closest to Chandler, brought him over to us. He had huge crocodile tears and snot running down his face. We consoled and cleaned him up before handing him over to his Mimi and proceeding with the questions. A couple minutes later, we heard the judge proclaim that he was so ordering the adoption of Chandler into our forever family. Applause broke out throughout the courtroom, even though most people sitting in the room were in the midst of brokenness in their own lives.

This scene reflects God's favor in so many ways. The gift of a new son, the love and support of friends and family, and the approval of the state, CPS, and attorneys for us to adopt Chandler all reflect His amazing grace and favor.

Experiencing that moment in the courtroom where so many others were there for very different reasons was sobering for me. It is only by God's grace that I was never in a courtroom like this one for a divorce proceeding. Instead, I was in this courtroom because of a new and blessed relationship with my new son. That is favor, favor that only God can grant.

CHAPTER 20

THE FATHER'S HEART FULFILLED

When I began writing this book, I outlined a chapter about "Letting Go", because I really thought that Chandler was going to return to someone in his family at any time. From the very day he arrived at our home, I thought it would be just a matter of days before he would leave our family. People asked me all the time how we were able to handle the emotional roller coaster of not knowing what Chandler's future held. It always gave me an opportunity to speak of God's grace in my life as He gave me the ability to see myself as Chandler's father no matter how long he was with us. Even in those days of uncertainty, God constantly fulfilled my father's heart. As I reflect on the 15 months from the time when Chandler came into our home until the day we adopted him, I have many fond memories of how my father's heart was being fulfilled.

One such memory took place one day when I was hanging out with Chandler. Danielle usually took care of him during the day, but because we both had flexible schedules, I would take care of Chandler anytime Danielle had to be away from home. She had a haircut appointment, so I spent a few hours with Chandler. He was about 14 months old at the time, so he had been with us for about six months—definitely long enough for us to be bonded. It was raining outside, but we needed to get out of the house, so we went to a local mall to play at an indoor toddler playground. Chandler was beginning to say a few words, and it was becoming apparent that he was very social. By the time he was walking, he was hugging anyone that came across his path. It did not matter if they were young or old, he felt that they all needed and wanted his hug. He is still like that, and it does not have to be people. He thinks that all dogs, cats, birds, Elmo, you name it, they all need a hug. We were walking into the mall, and he was excited to go play. We walked through a department store when Chandler greeted a salesperson, "Hi!" Then she joyfully responded back with, "Hello!" Chandler motioned back to me as I pushed his stroller and said, "Dada." The woman exclaimed, "How wonderful!" The brief interaction brought a smile to my face. It seemed completely normal.

After playing for a while, we went to the food court to get a bite to eat. As we sat at the table eating and watching people, Chandler began caressing my arm and pulling my hand to his chest to hug me. It did not matter to me who else was around. In that moment, this was my son loving on his daddy, and I can say without hesitation that I truly felt like his daddy. That was fulfilling as a father.

When it was unclear what Chandler's future held, I cherished every little opportunity like this to be his father. I knew that there was a very real possibility that I would never get to throw a baseball with him, or take him to his first day of school, or see him in a school play, or teach him how to drive, or meet his first date. However, I did get to hear him call me Dada, ask for countless hugs, and get excited when he got to ride with me in my truck or play outside with me. I got to see him light up when I picked him up from childcare at church, and I got to console him when he got hurt. Those moments alone would have been enough to fulfill my heart. My wife shared with me one night how she felt blessed to have finally been able to be a mom even if it would have ended up being only for a year or so. I felt exactly the same way about being a father.

Even if we had not been able to adopt Chandler, I would have felt a deep sense of fulfillment. I would have had the blessing of being his father for more than a year. When it began to look like we could possibly adopt Chandler, I was amazed at how my desire to be his father intensified. I think it was because my relationship with him was shifting in my mind, adjusting to the real possibility of being his father forever.

My friend John told me another story. When John and Leslie had their first child, John's mother and other friends and family were in the waiting room standing next to the door listening for the baby's cry. After the baby boy was birthed and everything was in order, John entered the waiting room. The first words out of John's mother's mouth were, "Now you know how much you can love a child." John and Leslie went on to have another son whom they love just as much. Then years later, they adopted a young teenage boy who had been in the foster system for several years. John shared with me, with tears in his eyes, that he has the exact same feeling of love for his adopted son as he does for his two biological sons. I, too, now know how much I can love a child.

Fulfilling the heart of Father God

Can you imagine how Father God must feel when we simply hang out with Him and love on Him? If my heart as a foster father is fulfilled when Chandler returns my love, how much more is God's heart fulfilled when we return His love? I also imagine that as God watched Chandler and I bond, that fulfilled Him as well.

One day I was having lunch with a pastor friend of mine. We were talking about Chandler and the journey that my wife and I had been on as foster parents. He asked me how the love and heart that I have for Chandler as a father reflected God's heart as a Father to us. I loved his question, but at that moment, I was not sure how to answer it. However, after that day at the mall, I knew at least part of the answer. At that time, I was 51, almost six feet tall, close to 200 pounds; college-educated, financially stable, and had traveled to many places around the world. In comparison to Chandler, I was far beyond his comprehension, strength, knowledge, and even awareness. Yet there I was spending time with him, focused on him, when I could have been doing a million other "more important" things. I was totally content to be with him. Even though God is omnipresent and omniscient and we are not, His desire to just be with us is much the same. Even though He is so much bigger, stronger, more intelligent, wealthy, and beyond our comprehension and even our awareness, He meets us every single time we look for Him. Jesus even told a story that described God as a Father who runs to us when we look for Him. God runs to meet with me? That is incredible. I know that His heart is filled when we return His love. Like any father, His heart is fulfilled when we emulate Him, long to be with Him, caress His loving arm. I hope you know Him like that, because I believe with all my heart that He looks upon you like that.

Change of Destiny

I not only have a fulfilled father's heart, I now also have a father's role to fulfill. Because my heart is full of love and compassion for Chandler, I desire the best for him. That is only natural for any loving father. This will have a profound impact on Chandler's destiny. Now that Chandler is our adopted son, his destiny is forever changed. This is not a negative reflection of his biological family. It is simply a fact, neither positive nor negative. Chandler obviously has not inherited any physical genetics from Danielle or me, but his destiny has been completely altered by our family. What he now will inherit emotionally and spiritually is drastically different from what he would have inherited from his biological family.

When we began to correspond with our adoption lawyer, we were sent some paperwork to fill out. One of the questions asked was whether or not we wanted to change Chandler's name. We knew that we wanted to keep his first name the same since he already knew himself by this name. (If you will remember, I am not using his real name in this book.) And we knew that we would change his last name to ours. We were going to keep his middle name the same, but then we noticed that it was the same as his biological father's. It was not a common name, so we concluded that it was a family name. Out of a desire to change his heritage, we decided to also change his middle name. This was not a small decision. We wanted to choose a name that would have meaning. Of course, like most parents, we were also paying attention to what sounded good. We first were considering Nathaniel, which had a meaning of "gift from

God." Chandler certainly was a gift from God to us. But we began to consider names that would have more of a bearing on Chandler. We were looking for a name that would either reflect his character or give him a heritage. We finally decided on Christopher, which means "bearer of Christ."

Bearer of Christ. I have no way of knowing what would have happened with Chandler in respect to becoming a Christ follower if he had remained with his biological family. Of course, we will never know. Indeed, there is no guarantee of that even with him being in our family now, but I believe that as his earthly father, I have great influence on this outcome. As I pray over Chandler each day, I ask God to call him to Himself at a young age. My prayer is that Chandler will fall deeply in love with his Heavenly Father as he seems to have with his earthly father. God is the One from whom Chandler receives his real destiny and identity. It is my desire and hope that he truly will become a bearer of Christ. Even at his young age, I can tell that he will grow up to influence other people. He loves people. He wants to be around people. He talks to everyone, young and old.

Some friends of ours babysat for us recently and told us a story about Chandler. Our friend had helped out with child care at church one Monday morning during a Mother of Preschoolers program. Chandler was in her classroom. She commented on how well he interacted with the other children. He seemed to want to help the other children whenever they were crying or upset. He was also able to communicate clearly with his words with the adults in the room. She described him as if he was more capable of comprehending his surroundings than many of his peers.

I have no doubt that Chandler will either influence people with the love and presence of Christ or he will influence them in other, not-so-beneficial ways. I choose to not leave that to chance. I believe that God is in control of Chandler's destiny, especially as I intercede on his behalf. As Chandler's adoptive father, I choose to ask God for a destiny that not only changes Chandler's life, but also the destiny of those with whom he comes in contact.

What a joy to be chosen to be Chandler's forever father. I am excited to be able to see him grow up and become a young man. Because I am more than 50 years older than Chandler, I do not know how much of his life I will be able to be a part of on this earth, but I know that I will cherish every moment, good or bad, fun or challenging.

The thought of that greatly fulfills my heart as a father!

CHAPTER 21
GOD'S FINGERPRINTS

L ittle did Danielle and I know that when we were sitting in that conference in February 2010 that Chandler would be born to young, unwed parents in October 2010. If you do the math, that means that while we were at that conference, Chandler's mother was just a few weeks pregnant. In fact, she might not even have known yet that she was pregnant. She may have even found out that she was pregnant about the same time the Holy Spirit was impressing on our hearts to begin the journey of becoming foster parents. She very well might have considered abortion, but thankfully did not choose that path. Being young and unmarried, she could have chosen to give her baby up for private adoption as soon as it was born, but instead she decided to try and raise her son. We do not know why she made that decision, and I am sad that neither she nor anyone else in Chandler's family was able or willing to care for him. However, I do not believe in fate. Rather, I believe in a God that directs the paths of people, both believers and non-believers, to accomplish His plan. We will never know this side of heaven exactly what His plan was in this incident, but the way things have turned out, it has God's fingerprints all over it.

There have only been a handful of times when I felt so strongly that God was speaking to my heart that it crowded out every other thought, and I even had a physical sensation.

The first time was the summer after my sophomore year in high school. To this day I can remember being at a youth camp and spending some time in prayer all alone one afternoon. I clearly and distinctly felt God was telling me to be involved in ministry. That moment has shaped my life from that day forward. The second time was November 1, 1987. That was the day I asked Danielle to marry me. We had gone to her apartment after church that Sunday to eat some lunch. After lunch, we knelt on her living room floor, held hands and began to pray. I was looking into her beautiful blue eyes, and it was as if God shoved a billboard into my tiny brain: "ASK HER TO MARRY YOU!" Yes, I asked her. I have reflected on that moment many times throughout our marriage, which has sustained me during challenging times. The third time was in February 2007. We had just returned home after leading a team on a mission trip to Thailand. By May 2007, we were making plans to move over to Thailand to volunteer for six months as missionaries. That decision, too, has shaped our future since that day. It continues to affect how I choose to live life today. It even played a large part in the fourth time that I have felt God speaking to my heart so clearly. The fourth time is when we were sitting at the conference in February 2010.

I am so thankful that we listened to what God was saying to us that day. I am also glad that we followed up on how we felt He was leading us even though it did not seem to dovetail with what we thought He wanted to do next in our lives. I am glad that we stayed the course when it took longer than I thought it would to become certified. We could have easily shut down after the not-so-good news from our home study. But again, I see God's providential hand in that, because if we had remained set on straight adoption only, we never would have fostered Chandler. If we had never fostered Chandler, we wouldn't have had the opportunity to adopt him, and this book would have had a much different ending. Then even after we decided to foster children, we had several opportunities to foster other children, but did not. It sure seems like to me that God had a plan for us to become a family.

A few weeks after we had adopted Chandler, Danielle showed me a card that she had bought for me for my 50th birthday. She had forgotten to give it to me. At first, I could not remember what we had done for my 50th birthday, which had been more than a year before. You'd think that a landmark birthday like one's 50th is a pretty easy one to remember. I still cannot remember what we did for my birthday, but

I remember the best gift I could have possibly received. Chandler had been placed with us just two weeks before my 50th birthday. Now *that* I will never forget!

As I write this final chapter, it has been almost three months since the day we adopted Chandler. It has been almost three years since we decided to pursue this path. What an adventure! Chandler is experiencing his second Christmas with us. This time, I am watching him through such a different lens. Last Christmas I wondered if that would be my last one with him. This year I am discussing with Danielle which Christmas traditions we want to begin as a family.

Because I see Chandler so much as my own flesh and blood now, I sometimes forget that not too long ago a complete stranger picked him up at daycare. That stranger brought him to our home, a completely strange place for him. Now it is no longer a strange place. It is his home. And we are not complete strangers to him. We are his mommy and daddy.

We have decided to spend the next several months getting used to being a new family. However, I still feel the tug to see what God has in store for us next. Will we foster another child? I really do not know yet, but I am sure that we will continue to find ways to meet the needs of some of the most vulnerable among us.

My prayer is that through this book, God is speaking to your heart, calling you to adopt His Father's heart. I encourage you to go back and read the chapter, "The Call of a Father's Heart." Then ask Him how you can respond to His call. There are many ways other than fostering or adopting. I suggest beginning by making it a priority to intercede on behalf of those who are orphaned both locally and around the world. This will help your heart get in tune with God's heart. Allow Him to speak to you. He might point you toward international organizations, such as Compassion International[7] or World Vision.[8] You may feel pulled toward a local children's home where you can build a close relationship with a child who lives at the home. You might have friends or family

---

[7] http://www.compassion.com

[8] http://www.wvi.org/wvi/wviweb.nsf

who are fostering, and you become certified so that you can provide respite care for that family. Perhaps you might learn about programs like CASA, Court Appointed Special Advocate. CASA trains volunteers to become advocates for foster children. This advocate is appointed to a child for the entire time the child is in CPS care. The CASA volunteer's only focus is the best interest of that child. They become an advocate for that child in court and usually have great influence on decisions that are made regarding that child.[9]

For me, God's call to have a father's heart for the orphan is undeniable. The fact is that there are many, many ways to step into that calling.

The big question is whether you will respond—or ignore that call.

---

[9]   http://www.casaforchildren.org/site/c.mtJSJ7MPIsE/b.5301295/k.BE9A/ Home.htm